YOU

EVERYTHING YOU NEED *to* MASTER

GOT

AUTHENTIC PUBLIC SPEAKING

THIS

LISA KLEIMAN

RIVER GROVE
BOOKS

Published by River Grove Books
Austin, TX
www.rivergrovebooks.com

Distributed by River Grove Books

Design and composition by Greenleaf Book Group
Cover design by Greenleaf Book Group
Cover image: Mircrophone, Azat Valeev. Used under license from Shutterstock.com

Publisher's Cataloging-in-Publication data is available.

Print ISBN: 978-1-63299-232-1

eBook ISBN: 978-1-63299-233-8

First Edition

This book is dedicated to my husband and daughter. I'm grateful for their encouragement and patience, and especially for allowing me the nonjudgmental space to work on and complete it.

I would also like to dedicate this book in loving memory to my late nephew, Michael, who infused soulful and creative writing and illustrations of a book that was yet to be published. This book is in honor of your quest.

CONTENTS

Preface

Sitting in my high school English class at age seventeen, feeling nauseous in anticipation of my turn to stand up in front of the class and give a formal presentation about a famous historical author, I never would have guessed that I'd spend many years of my life helping others improve their public speaking skills, especially in the role of instructor. The idea of speaking in front of an audience as a profession seemed awful. I didn't understand why people would want to purposely expose themselves to possible ridicule and embarrassment. I dreaded giving speeches in class and almost didn't run for a student council position because I was fearful of giving the required "vote for me" speech to the entire student body. (I was subsequently very relieved and surprised when I won.) In hindsight, part of that fear could have stemmed from an age-related environment conducive to judgment—teens judging others and themselves—especially those in authority.

This fear carried on through college. I panicked at the thought of giving a speech in front of a class. Fortunately, or so I thought at the time, few courses I took required such an assignment. Following college, the next several years were spent on developing a career, mostly in the corporate world. I still carried that self-inflicted fear with me, always hoping I wouldn't have to give a presentation, but I admired those who could dynamically articulate their message in front of a live audience.

One speaker stood out to me in particular. I had attended an all-day off-site business writing workshop and was captivated by one of the presenters. She seemed so passionate and charged about her role, and that drew me in. I wanted to experience that feeling as well and be like her, oddly thinking that maybe speaking in front of people and being that engaging *would* be something I'd like to do.

As time progressed, I gained more experience with giving presentations, mostly in work situations and in various professional organizations. Even though giving presentations was not a primary function of roles I held early in my career, I still had to periodically speak in front of a group, such as when presenting results, updates, or proposals to management and staff; leading department meetings; negotiating formally with clients; training staff; and networking. Initially I found these experiences nerve-wracking, especially if I felt inferior to others—those I thought had more prestige and business experience than I did. My high school self would come creeping back, worried I was being judged. However, over time I became more confident and ultimately more comfortable giving presentations. I actually grew to enjoy them. Eventually I took on instructing and training roles, which mainly involved speaking in front of an audience.

I have now coached individuals and facilitated hundreds of classes, workshops, and seminars for diverse audiences across the globe on such topics as public speaking, business writing, business communication, English as a second language, and English composition through my roles in management and consulting positions at private organizations and Fortune 500 companies and as a lecturer for higher learning at various universities and adult education organizations.

Today I embrace public speaking opportunities. I get excited when asked to speak in front of a group, no matter the size. Admittedly, I still feel some trepidation prior to the presentation, some worry about failure. However, I know those thoughts are constructive, because I want to do well. Even if I still have a few flutters that well up in my stomach just prior to speaking, a switch turns on as soon as I set foot on the stage. I feel elated and charged, and my mind instantly switches gears to focus on the audience instead of on how I'm feeling. I have learned to approach public speaking with strategies that work. The public speaking journey can be rewarding; it's an accomplishment to give a speech, which will likely include mixed emotions of relief that it's over and the satisfaction of knowing that you had the courage to complete it.

I was inspired to write this book to help others learn how to present as easily and smoothly as possible. My journey in becoming a confident, polished speaker took many years; much of it was by trial and error. I could have benefited from using a resource that showed me how to plan and what to do to pull off a good speech. Thinking back to presentations I'd given years ago, there were many I did not feel good about; I was frustrated, not knowing how to get started or how to convey my message. At times I rambled for too long, never quite getting to the point. Other times I didn't say enough, or I didn't clearly communicate the purpose of my speech, leaving my audience confused and likely annoyed. I needed a step-by-step explanation of what to do not only when preparing a speech, but also what to do when things don't go as planned during a speech.

I spent many hours learning what I could about public speaking, sometimes for unique and specific occasions, such as when introducing or honoring a guest speaker. I asked other speakers for advice, viewed recordings of various related speeches, attended presentations and assessed the speakers, and read whatever I could find about speaking publicly. I learned a lot in the process, and it took a lot of time. This book provides a resource for many of these things. My hope is that you won't have to spend countless hours, as I did, to become a better public speaker. This book is intended to be a "one-stop" resource, a quick reference tool, for becoming a solid public speaker, no matter the occasion and purpose. My goal is for you to enjoy giving speeches.

the important activity and the need to help others strengthen their ability to communicate in this way. Seeing them challenge their credibility and gain confidence at speaking in public inspired me to push myself in strengthening my ability to help others build their public speaking skills.

Acknowledgments

The content for this book is based on a conglomeration of resources that includes personal experience, research, and shared stories from those who can attest to and advise about public speaking. I'm grateful to those whose speaking engagement experiences provided fodder for examples that I share in this book and for those who have meticulously studied and published their work about public speaking. When gathering information for this book, I pleasantly found that people willingly shared, when asked, their public speaking experiences. Most would quickly remember what they considered embarrassing moments, or their fears, when presenting publicly, and they didn't hesitate to offer advice on some tricks of the trade.

There was a common theme about public speaking—it's unavoidable, and it's an activity that can put us at risk because it affects our credibility and professional standing. This risk is why so many prefer to, and even go to great lengths to, avoid public speaking, even to the extent of labeling themselves as not being good at it. Conversely, this risk is also what sets people apart. Those who take the risk and challenge it can propel their careers. I wish to thank the thousands of students and the many clients I've had the pleasure of working with to develop their public speaking skills. They've helped me understand more about this important activity and the need to help others strengthen their ability to communicate in this way. Seeing them challenge their vulnerabilities and gain confidence at speaking in public inspired me to push myself in strengthening my ability to help others build their public speaking skills.

A final thanks to all who helped make this book happen.

Introduction

Speaking in front of a live audience is pretty much inescapable. Even if you do your best to avoid it, you'll likely still find yourself in some situation where you are formally telling a public audience about something—yourself, your business, or some other subject. Some people *love* speaking in front of a live audience. But most people don't like and even fear speaking formally in public, especially when they're worried that their credibility is at stake and it's important that the presentation go well.

If you truly love public speaking, I applaud you. I would also love to talk to you and find out what inspires you about this activity and how you came to enjoy it—because you are a minority. Many have *learned* that public speaking can enhance their career and confidence and can even be an energizing adrenaline rush, but public speaking is known for sparking fear. Type in any version of "why people enjoy public speaking" in any major online search engine, and you'll get a list of topics addressing the fear, not the enjoyment, of public speaking. It seems that fear often dampens any excitement about an activity that can produce very positive outcomes.

Or you may not enjoy public speaking, but you don't necessarily fear it either, and you prefer not to do it because you think it can take too much work to be able to present well. Preparing for giving a speech involves planning, creating, and rehearsing, and you may have to travel to and from the event. It's a commitment to present with integrity. Is it worth it? You decide. (This book is designed to help you do all that as easily and effectively as possible.)

Or you might be someone who truly doesn't like speaking in public. Some fear is normal and can be helpful to presenting well, but not if the fear is so consuming that you avoid it at all costs. The fear of public speaking is called *glossophobia*. Studies show that many people have a heightened fear of engaging with others in a variety of social interaction. Mental Health America reports that social anxiety affects approximately 15 million or 7 percent of American adults.[1] Whether you get anxiety at just the thought of public speaking, or experience full-on panic, you can overcome the unpleasant experience through learning how to embrace and use fear productively.

WHY YOU SHOULD BE A PUBLIC SPEAKER

I've asked thousands of adults, either in casual conversation or formally surveying students in college courses, what communication skill they would most like to improve. The majority state public speaking, often followed by a definitive description supporting their answer. Many people feel tense, nervous, and uncomfortable when giving a speech. However, often these same people—which include those just out of high school to those with decades of work and life experience—quickly improve and feel much better about speaking publicly after learning and applying some basic tools. I've seen countless people go from being petrified at the thought of presenting to elation after discovering their newly developed public speaking skills and realizing that they *can* present with confidence. Thus, the impetus for this book is to provide tools anyone can apply, regardless of their skills and

---

1   "Social Anxiety Disorder," Anxiety and Depression Association of America, http://www.adaa.org/understanding-anxiety/social-anxiety-disorder.

experience, to easily present in any situation. There are so many benefits to mastering this skill. You can:

- **Learn to communicate ideas effortlessly.** The more you speak publicly, the more skilled you'll get at it. In time, you can easily voice your ideas and share information in diverse settings.

- **Improve your organizational skills.** You'll develop strong organizational skills. A well-planned speech involves research, writing, and overall organization of your content—a practice applicable to any personal and professional activity.

- **Succeed at work.** Speaking up in meetings, promoting your ideas, and presenting yourself as a professional can help you stand out at work, impress clients, and excel in job interviews.

- **Gain instant authority.** As a speaker, you're instantly thought of as an authority. Whether you're speaking to ten or five hundred people, you have a platform that inherently elicits respect. This role can be powerful, and you can influence others, especially if you nail your performance.

- **Speak effectively to diverse audiences.** You'll learn to speak to diverse audiences, preventing any cultural barriers and faux pas.

- **Inspire others.** You can become a powerful means of helping and inspiring people to help themselves.

- **Improve your fluency and articulation.** You'll refine your voice and improve your vocabulary, learning what to say and how to say it. Understanding how your messages affect others also helps build confidence.

- **Pull off an effective impromptu speech.** When asked to speak on the spot, without preparation, you'll calmly accept the offer and feel more at ease in presenting fluidly.

- **Increase your professional network.** Going to any conference or professional type of event is a great way to meet people and expand your professional network. However, going to such an event as a speaker, putting yourself "out there" with confidence, will boost your chance of success even more. You'll find that people will eagerly want to talk to you.

- **Expand your career opportunities.** Employers look for and hire people who can communicate well. A 2017 survey by the National Association of Colleges and Employers found that the ability to communicate effectively is the quality employers most want to see in new recruits.

- **Build confidence.** You'll learn to make eye contact and speak confidently to anyone in practically any situation, benefiting you in your personal and professional activities.

WHAT TO EXPECT FROM THIS BOOK

Despite what you may think, you *can* learn to be a powerful public speaker, and this book provides the tools necessary to deliver a strong speech. You'll learn to:

- Considerably reduce presentation anxiety
- Design strategies for engaging your audience
- Be authentic when you present
- Deliver engaging presentations on camera and online
- Present effectively at a variety of venues to large or small audiences
- Deliver impromptu speeches with ease and finesse
- Comfortably and confidently deliver strong, short persuasive pitches

- Structure and organize a clear, attention-grabbing message that your audience will remember
- Effectively plan, manage, and address audience questions with success
- Know when and how to smoothly adapt your message during your speech

The journey to becoming a dynamic public speaker can be fun and rewarding. The more you do it, the easier it will get, and you'll gain confidence with each step.

HOW TO USE THIS BOOK

This book is designed for you to choose what to read, in any order, applicable to your interest and needs. I encourage you to start with the sections where you need the most work. Here's a breakdown of how the material is organized.

Part 1: Getting started—planning

Part 1 (Chapters 1–5) covers the planning stages of a presentation. It describes vital aspects and factors that affect any presentation, such as the audience, medium, and venue, that should be considered before developing the speech. Without a good plan, a speech may not go as well as intended. This section applies to any kind of speech.

Part 2: Building your presentation

Part 2 (Chapters 6–9) addresses building your speech. It provides guidance on writing the purpose, outline, beginning, middle, and end, as well as instructions for targeting your speech to your audience.

Part 3: Fine-tuning your presentation

Part 3 (Chapters 10–14) is about how to fine-tune your speech once you have your basic outline nailed down and you know what you want to say and in what order. It also addresses the visual aspect of a speech, specifically visual aids, including why, when, and how to apply them effectively so they enhance a presentation. This section also applies to any type of speech.

Part 4: Putting it all together

Part 4 (Chapters 15–16) addresses how to polish and refine the presentation and includes practicing and preparing or setting up an event or live presentation on the internet.

Part 5: Delivery

Part 5 (Chapters 17–18) describes effective strategies for using your voice and body language. It includes tips on how to reduce and eliminate filler words and ways to use body movements to enhance your speech. These chapters will help you understand how to develop a delivery strategy.

Part 6: Types of speeches

Part 6 (Chapters 19–27) addresses the different types of speeches, including those that occur during employment interviews, weddings, and award and anniversary events and those that occur online. Elevator and impromptu speeches are also covered as well as how to effectively present to small and large groups.

Part 7: Strategies for a great speech

Part 7 (Chapters 28–34) addresses success strategies for public speaking. These chapters cover a broad category of potentially challenging circumstances, including public speaking fear and stage fright, audience questions, resistant and challenging audience participants, and overall presentation mishaps. These chapters also detail ways to use meditation as a successful speech strategy and how to use humor and props during a speech. Additionally, this section highlights well-known speakers, describing how and why they learned to present, helping you understand how others have learned to do it well.

Conclusion

The conclusion provides a list of ways you can tell that your speech has been a success.

PART 1

Getting Started— Planning

"If you don't know what you want to achieve in your presentation, your audience never will."

—Harvey Diamond

Getting Started—Planning

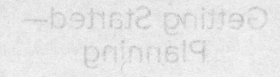

—Harvey Diamond

Have you ever had to give a public speech but weren't sure how to get started? You may have agonized over the topic, wondering what topic you should even speak about, let alone try to put together a complete speech.

Perhaps you thought you had planned sufficiently for a presentation but didn't, experiencing a less than ideal result.

Planning is a vital component for a successful speech. Taking the time to effectively plan can make it easier to develop and present powerfully.

In general, you'll need to address these five elements, described in detail in the following chapters, to plan a successful presentation:

1. The purpose of your speech

2. Your audience

3. The venue or location

4. The time and length of your presentation

5. The method of presenting

CHAPTER 1

Know Your Purpose

You won't achieve what you want if you don't
know what you want.

The first step in planning a speech is to identify why you're making the presentation. Think through what you want to achieve and what you want your audience to get out of the presentation. Knowing your goal from the beginning will help you with the design, tone, organization, and administration of your presentation. To get started, answer these four questions:

1. What is the goal of my speech?
2. What do I want my audience to know?
3. What do I want my audience to do with the information I am providing?
4. What do I hope to achieve?

WHAT IS THE GOAL OF MY SPEECH?

Start by identifying your goal and focus on what you want to accomplish. Ask yourself why you're presenting and how it's meaningful for you and your audience. Consider also whether you want to inform, persuade, or entertain the audience.

WHAT DO I WANT MY AUDIENCE TO KNOW?

Next, identify what you want your audience to understand, learn, or do. For example, perhaps you want your audience to learn how to do something or learn about something new.

WHAT DO I WANT MY AUDIENCE TO DO WITH THE INFORMATION I AM PROVIDING?

After you've established what knowledge you are bestowing on your audience, consider whether you want them to act on this information, and if so, how. For example, if you want your audience to volunteer their time for a cause you are promoting, you could send them a sign-up form by email, a link through social media, or pass around a sign-up sheet during or after your presentation. You could place the sign-up sheet on a table near the door where the audience will exit. Your method will depend on the location and audience.

WHAT DO I HOPE TO ACHIEVE?

Assess what you want to ultimately get out of the presentation. You may want to build your credibility, garner support for a cause, or get funding for a start-up business. Consider why it's worth the time and energy (and pressure or anxiety) to deliver a speech.

Here's a simple example: Let's say that Mia, a sales representative for a clothing wholesaler, has been asked by her boss to give a presentation about the current trends in casual and lifestyle clothing at an upcoming apparel and accessories trade show. Mia's company plans to be an exhibitor at the show to grow brand awareness and establish new accounts. In planning her speech, Mia considers these questions:

- What is the purpose of my speech?
  - The purpose of Mia's speech is to educate retailers about current trends in fashion.
- What do I want my audience to know?
  - Mia will want the audience to know which merchandise is a good investment.
- What do I want my audience to do with the information?
  - Mia wants the audience to know the type of merchandise they should purchase.
- What do I hope to achieve?
  - Mia hopes to inspire retailers to purchase from her company.

Knowing the answers to these questions, no matter what your own presentation is about, will help you outline and organize your speech, and you'll be able to tailor your speech to your purpose. In Mia's case, her next steps may include adding details that better address and support her purpose. For example, she may need to address demand, the competition, application, and availability of the product.

(i) TIP

Consider your general purpose first. For example, do you want to sell or inform, or do you want to seek information from your audience? Next, draft an objective, possibly identifying one thing that you want your audience to think, feel, or do.

If you're asked to present, make sure you understand the reasons for the request. Find out the purpose of the presentation from the person or organization who asked you to speak:

- What would you like me to talk about?
- What are your/company/audience expectations for the presentation?
- What do you want your audience to get out of the presentation?
- Why did you ask me to present?

I recommend documenting the answers, so you can refer to them as needed to stay on track as you develop your speech. You don't want to lose sight of what was asked of you.

the presentation?

CHAPTER 2

Know Your Audience

Take the time to learn about your
prospective audience.

I f you want your presentation to be well received, it must be interesting and engaging, and this means knowing something about
your audience. Knowing about your audience's interests and their
knowledge of your topic helps you understand how to draft and target your message. A speech about basic photography would likely
bore an audience of experienced photographers. However, a speech
about a high-tech camera that's new to the market could interest
professional photographers who might want to purchase this product. No one wants to sit through a long speech about something
they have no interest in, don't see or understand the value of, that's
too simplistic or too technical, or addresses content they perceive as
personally offensive.

TIP

An effective presentation takes full consideration of the audience needs to capture their interest, develop their understanding, inspire their confidence, and achieve the presenter's objectives.

Learn as much as you can about your audience, such as their age, culture, education and economic status, work experience, needs and concerns, interests, rapport (with you), and expectations. Consider how these factors may affect how you should communicate your ideas. For example, if you were going to talk to a teenage audience about the dangers of drinking and driving, then age would be an important factor in how you convey that message. In this case, showing images of crashes caused by drunk drivers might be more impactful than presenting a detailed table or bar chart of crash statistics.

Considering your audience also applies to any presentations you post on the internet. For example, if you want to post a video presentation about dog obedience training (to promote your dog obedience services business), then you need to understand how you can best reach potential customers (i.e., which social media platform, if applicable) and captivate their interest. (Of course, some presentations posted online spread like wildfire, quickly reaching the masses—despite the presenter not knowing much about who views them.)

Address these questions to learn about your audience:

- Who is my direct audience?
- Who will be affected by the message?
- What is my relationship to the audience?
- How will my audience respond to the message?
- What does my audience need to know?

- What do I want the audience to do with the information?
- How do I want the audience to feel about my message?

METHODS TO COLLECT DATA ABOUT YOUR AUDIENCE

You may already know a good bit about your audience, especially if they're people you know well, such as family members and friends or those you work with regularly. However, if you don't know who will be attending your presentation, there are methods of finding out what you can about them.

Online surveys

Require those who sign up to attend your presentation to fill out a survey. Whether it's online or some other format, include questions that will reveal information to help you tailor your speech to your audience. You might ask about their interest in your topic, their age, their education, or their financial situation. What can you ask about their demographic that might tell you something about what they want to know and learn? Keep in mind, though, that people may be turned off by completing any kind of online survey, so you may need to include a promotional incentive.

Face-to-face interview

By talking to people face-to-face and getting information directly from them, you'll also be able to observe their nonverbal language. You'll be able to revise your questions as needed, getting direct and possibly more specific responses. Respondents will also have more time to consider their answers and provide you with more detailed insight.

Research

You can always glean information about your audience through secondary information. For example, when speaking to members of a specific organization, such as Habitat for Humanity or the American Advertising Federation, visiting their website and any related and applicable third-party sources could reveal insights about the goals, activities, and beliefs of the organization. A quick internet search is an easy way to find out about your audience.

Site analytics

If you already have online content, such as a website, consider reviewing the data you have available to you about your visitors. Some analytic tools tell you where your visitors are coming from and which of your topics and pages get the most traffic. Some track what customers are doing on your page, such as their mouse movements and how far down the page they scroll. There are plenty of tools out there that collect user information, thus giving you insight into your unique web visitors. This can be very helpful when you're trying to figure out where your audience's interests lie.

Experience based

If direct information about your audience is limited, use your personal experience to consider characteristics, beliefs, and motives your audience might have. For example, you may have already presented the same speech to a similar audience. You could also speak with people who may be like the type of people attending your speech and ask them for information. You could do the same with your audience before you begin your presentation, spending some time meeting and greeting people, introducing yourself, and asking about them. Connecting with your audience before you present has the added benefit of creating legitimacy and rapport with the group.

BE CAREFUL ABOUT STEREOTYPING

Avoid classifying everyone into one group; beware of preconceived notions. A thorough audience analysis will help you refine and better understand your audience's interests, goals, and knowledge of your topic, but fixing beliefs and opinions about people neglects possible individual differences, resulting in flawed reasoning of the audience overall. The best way to avoid incorrect stereotyping is to learn as much as you can about your audience rather than making assumptions, and rely on varying sources of information.

CONTINUE TO ANALYZE THE AUDIENCE

An audience analysis doesn't just happen during the planning stages of a presentation. It can be done during the presentation as well. Continue to get feedback from your audience as you go through your speech. When giving a live presentation, you may want to revise your approach on the spot if you notice that your audience appears bored or confused. Depending on your audience, you might have to provide necessary explanations or background information to clarify ideas, or you may have to pull out some tricks to get the audience better engaged and more alert.

APPROACH

A speech to an audience you already know well might be a different speech than one to people you've never met before. You'll likely use a less formal approach when speaking to colleagues and a more formal approach when speaking to potential investors or new customers.

The following is a worksheet you may find helpful for understanding your audience. When planning your presentation, I recommend filling out as much information on this worksheet as possible. The better you know your audience, the better you will be set up for success in giving your presentation.

Audience Analysis Worksheet
Presentation Planning: Who Is Your Audience?

AUDIENCE CRITERIA	NOTES
Average age	
Gender	
Profession	
Religion	
Personality type	
Interests	
Education level	
Primary language	
Peers, Superiors, Subordinates	
Group affiliations	
Language and cultural differences	
Interest in topic	
Knowledge of topic	
Attitude toward topic	
Values toward topic	
Familiarity of specialized terminology	
Familiarity and relationship with you	
Voluntary or mandatory attendance	

Continued

AUDIENCE CRITERIA	NOTES
Purpose of attending	
Method of attending	
Location/Time difference	
Preferred communication channel (I.e., social media, email, website, face-to-face, phone, etc.)	
Other	

CHAPTER 3

Know the Location

Find out as much as you can about the
location where you will present.

E arly on in my academic career, the university where I worked
assigned me to teach an evening course at a small military base
off-site. Due to the base's strict security, I wasn't allowed access
into the building to review the classroom prior to the first class. However,
I had taught the same course on campus in well-equipped classrooms.
I assumed that the room at the base where I would conduct the class
would be adequately set up for a teaching and learning environment.

I was excited to work with the military students and had several
activities prepared to keep the students engaged and active involving
the use of video and online content. I was ready, but my first day of
class didn't go as anticipated.

I arrived at the base about an hour before the evening class started,
so I had enough time to make copies, get all my materials set up,
and be prepared and ready when the students arrived. However, the

administration building where the copier was located was locked, and I couldn't find anyone around to help me. *No matter*, I thought; I could still proceed without the handouts. However, I soon found out that the only instructional tool available in the classroom was a chalkboard. There was no access to an internet connection or screen projection equipment. I had a lesson prepared for the entire three hours of the class that I couldn't use because I didn't have the technology and equipment needed. I also didn't have a plan B.

Fortunately, I knew the material well enough and had a few tricks up my sleeve for engaging the students. An hour and a half into the class, we took a fifteen-minute break. I was the only one who went outside for the break, not knowing that in the evening, the doors to exit the building automatically locked. I was locked out and had no way to contact the students to let me back in. After thirty minutes, a student finally came outside, planning to leave for the night because the class thought I had left and wasn't coming back! We both went back inside, and I explained to the class what had happened. They were sympathetic, but I could tell they weren't amused. They were tired, it was the end of a long day of work for them, and they understandably didn't want their time wasted.

Had I taken the time before the class started to learn as much as I could about the location of the classroom and resources, the outcome would have been different.

To prevent unexpected issues and deliver your speech with confidence, become familiar with the room and space where you'll be speaking. If possible, visit the place where you'll present so you can assess the environment and plan accordingly. Be aware of how you'll be entering and exiting the venue, and make sure any equipment you need for your presentation is available. If it's not, that's something you'll need to bring with you. Becoming familiar with your venue will help you anticipate and prevent any surprises when it's time for your presentation.

If you are presenting online, become familiar with the platform you'll be using to reach your target audience. Know the software well and have a backup plan for any issues. This is especially important if you will be presenting live, in real time, so you can manage the experience and address issues immediately. (See Chapter 25 for more details about presenting online.)

Take these steps to avoid potential issues during your presentation:

- **Do your own setup.** Don't rely completely on others to do this for you. By setting up for your presentation yourself, you'll have a better idea of what to expect and how to handle any unexpected mishaps during your speech. That stated, consider having others available who can quickly assist you with any issues if need be.

- **Test your timing at the location.** Even if you've practiced at home or in your office, practice at the location where you'll be presenting. You may find that your timing is different. Practicing at the location can also help boost your confidence.

- **Learn about the location.** Find out as much as possible about the location where you'll present. If you can't access the venue prior to your speech, ask someone at the facility for answers.

I've created the following worksheet to help you assess your presentation venue.

Onsite Presentation Location
Assessment Worksheet

ASSESSMENT CRITERIA	NOTES
Room capacity How many people will the event hold?	
Room size How big is the room?	
Availability of equipment What equipment will you have access to, including microphone, overhead projector, computer equipment, and extensions cords?	
Internet Is it fast or slow? What is the name of the network and password?	
Lighting Can the lights be dimmed? Are there spotlights, and if so where?	
Control of ambiance Are there curtains or blinds that you can adjust?	
Location of light and volume switches Will you have convenient access to light switches or will you require assistance?	
Noise distractions Can you hear noises from an adjacent hallway or room or from the outside?	
Location of parking Do you have to walk a long way from your car to the facility carrying equipment?	
Seating arrangement Are the seats tiered or fixed, and can you rearrange them?	
Platform Will you be presenting on a raised platform or at the same level as your audience?	
Refreshments Will there be refreshments and water provided where you're presenting?	

ASSESSMENT CRITERIA	NOTES
Your presentation location Will you be seated or standing during your presentation?	
Lectern or table Will there be a lectern or table on stage if needed?	
Multiple presenters If others are also presenting, will they be on the stage with you, and if so, where will they be?	
Handicap accessible Are there stairs and accommodations for the handicapped?	

CHAPTER 4

Consider Best Time and Length

What will you say about your topic in thirty seconds and in one hour?

As you prepare for your presentation, two things that are extremely important to keep in mind are the length of your speech and what time of day you will be presenting. Consider the following two scenarios:

Nicole had just finished a light breakfast before entering the auditorium at 10:00 a.m. She grabbed some coffee provided at the entrance and found a seat near the center front. She easily settled in and was ready for the presentation to begin. By 10:45 a.m., the presentation was over. Nicole was ready to get some lunch and think about all she had learned from the speaker.

About 11:30 a.m., one hour into the presentation he was attending, Ryan's stomach began growling. It would be another thirty minutes before the session would break for lunch. All he could focus on during that time was getting food, and soon!

Which scenario would you prefer your audience to experience: ready and alert or hungry and distracted? There are a variety of techniques and factors involved that affect audience engagement. Time of the day is one of them. Another is the length of your presentation. You want to present for an adequate amount of time to be able to convey your message, but if you go on for too long, your audience will stop paying attention to you. Here are four questions about time of day and length to consider when scheduling your speech.

WHICH TIME OF THE DAY IS BEST TO PRESENT?

If someone else asks you to speak, there's no flexibility regarding when you present. However, if you do have a choice, consider these optimal times: morning, midafternoon, and possibly weekends. If you're presenting online, any time will work.

Morning

If possible, present in the morning when people are usually the most alert, but avoid a late morning start because people may get hungry and focus on lunch instead of your speech. If you're presenting in the morning, you might want to plan your presentation to be over by at least 10:45 or 11:00 a.m.

*NOTE: The term *generally* is used for consideration of your audience. It's best to know as much as you can about who you're presenting to; that includes their customs, routines, and schedule. For example, your audience may be more alert later in the day or just before starting a later shift.

Afternoon

Early afternoon, just after lunch, may not be the best time to present because at this time of day people often feel sleepy and lethargic. However, midafternoon (about 1:30 to 3:30 p.m.) can be a good time. If you are presenting later than that, people may be thinking about getting home, negotiating traffic, running errands, and what to have for dinner, so you should avoid the late afternoon as well.

Evenings or weekends

Outside of normal working hours, especially on the weekend, people may be more receptive to a presentation because they want to be there as opposed to being required to be there. Evenings can be tricky, though. People may attend during this time because it's the only time they can go; however, they may feel tired and hungry and be less alert. So make sure your evening presentations are particularly engaging.

Online

People surf the web at all hours, so you never know who might come across your presentation at a particular time. It could be seen by anyone across time zones. So if you're presenting online, time of day is irrelevant. However, there are some things you should keep in mind regarding optimal times for online presentations. For example, your audience may be available to meet or attend online during work hours if they are viewing your presentation to further their career. Or they might be viewing your online presentation before or after work hours, when they are home and can watch your presentation on their laptop while cooking dinner. Let whatever your presentation is about inform this piece.

And don't forget to consider yourself as well. You want to be as alert as possible when presenting, so schedule your speech during a time of day when you would likely feel your best.

HOW WILL YOU ENGAGE YOUR AUDIENCE DURING LESS-THAN-OPTIMAL TIMES?

If you don't have an option of when to present and are stuck with a time that is less than optimal, don't fret. You can still pull off a great speech, regardless of the time of day it's given. Consider activities requiring audience participation to keep attendees alert and engaged (see Chapter 5 for more ideas) during times when they may have trouble staying focused on your presentation. For example, you could:

- Provide quick snacks and refreshments when presenting during times that your audience might be getting hungry
- Ask thought-provoking questions
- Give your audience a written task
- Take a brief five-minute break
- Make your video (live or recorded) presentation interactive so viewers can swipe, click, post comments, and engage with you or your video

ARE YOU ONE OF SEVERAL SPEAKERS?

If you aren't the only presenter, find out how many speakers will be presenting and review the schedule of events. If possible, request the time slot when you prefer to present. There are drawbacks to going last, as the audience may not be as attentive and the previous speakers may have run over their allotted time, leaving less left for you. However, being the last speaker may also mean that the audience will remember your speech rather than ones given earlier, so that is something to consider as well. No matter when you're scheduled on the lineup, don't go over your allotted time. That cuts into the time of the speakers following you, which is just poor etiquette.

HOW MUCH TIME ARE YOU ALLOWED FOR YOUR SPEECH?

Know how much time you've been allotted so you can plan your speech to include time for questions. Keep in mind that people find it difficult to concentrate for long periods of time. If your speech is longer than forty-five minutes, consider pausing for short breaks so you and your audience have time to recharge.

CHAPTER 5

Select the Method

What do you know about the event and
how you will give your speech?

I n a small conference room with a handful of subordinates, Andy shared results from a weak quarter. Sales were disappointing, and he wanted his staff to discuss possible solutions for improvement. He stood when giving his presentation; all attendees were silent and seemed focused on his words. Then he sat back down and encouraged the staff to speak up and brainstorm ideas.

Andy's strategy seemed to work. He appeared authoritative, commanding the attention of those seated. He wanted to ensure that his message was taken seriously. However, he also wanted his staff to relax and think freely about ideas. Sitting down placed him on an even keel with the group, creating a conducive environment for open discussion. His staff began to open up about their own ideas and suggestions, just as he hoped they would.

When developing your presentation, consider an appropriate delivery method for the material you plan to present. Will you stand or sit? Will you elicit audience participation? Will you use visual aids? If so, how will you manage them?

In this example, Andy could have presented differently, starting out his presentation seated and then seizing the moment and the authority by standing to emphasize a point. Either approach can work; it just depends on the desired outcome.

Your delivery depends on many factors, including the channel (i.e., online or on-site), the size of the venue, your comfort level with presenting, your familiarity with the topic, and the audience's expectations.

Considering these key aspects when planning your method of presenting will give you the best results.

AUDIENCE PARTICIPATION

To engage your audience, keep them active. For example, you could have them work on a task in groups or with the person sitting next to them. Getting your audience involved can work for almost any type of presentation event, online or on-site. Keep in mind seating arrangements, though, as fixed, theater-style seating is not conducive to having people get up and work in groups of three or more. However, in these settings you could have people interact individually or one-on-one. You might present your audience with a problem and ask them to write down possible solutions and then share them with the person sitting next to them.

THE OCCASION

A formal conference with several hundred people in attendance will require a different approach than a presentation to six of your colleagues, a speech at a wedding, or a talk given to clients in a video conference. For large venues, your role is likely to provide information, and you often will use visual aids, such as slides. However, for smaller audiences and venues, your presentation could be more of a discussion, where slides aren't appropriate. Tailoring your presentation to the occasion is key.

YOUR FAMILIARITY WITH THE AUDIENCE

A less-formal approach is typical for an audience of a few people who you know well. In these situations (such as for business meetings or workshops), handouts that summarize the key points may suffice. For larger, more formal presentations, especially if you don't know the audience, slides may be more appropriate. Your familiarity with the audience will also determine your tone. If you are presenting to people you know, your tone can be less formal and more conversational.

YOUR COMFORT LEVEL AND EXPERIENCE WITH PRESENTING

People who have little experience with speaking in public may not feel comfortable presenting without the use of notes. Even more experienced presenters, who may be able to adjust their speech on the spot as needed, may have notes available, or a teleprompter they can refer to. However, regardless of your experience, use notes only as a backup to jog your memory; don't use them as a crutch. Focusing most of your attention on a piece of paper instead of on the audience is something you want to avoid.

YOUR FAMILIARITY WITH THE TOPIC

Know as much as you can about your topic so you can more fluidly and energetically present it without relying on any detailed notes. (I highly discourage using detailed notes during your speech; you may end up reading aloud to your audience, possibly causing you to speak in a monotone instead of more authentically and naturally.) Being as knowledgeable as possible about your topic is a great way to be sure that you will present confidently, and your audience will be more likely to listen to what you have to say.

TIP

Start with what you know, and then research to learn more. Do this before deciding what you will say.

YOUR PERSONAL PRESENTATION PREFERENCES

Some people are more comfortable winging it on the spot without any kind of formal and thought-through planning and practice. Others prefer as much time as possible to plan, practice, and put together a polished, well-rehearsed speech. Longer talks will likely require planning and practice for best results. Shorter speeches, such as wedding toasts or congratulatory remarks, may work well when given impromptu, although it may be helpful to plan and practice for these as well. Whatever your preferences, make sure you know your own abilities and comfort level.

PRESENTATION METHODS

Taking the time to understand the factors involved with your presentation will help you make the best decision about what method to use. The website skillsyouneed.com offers guidelines based on formality of the occasion. Use the following chart to help you get started.

Presentation Methods Guide

	VERY FORMAL	FORMAL	INFORMAL	VERY INFORMAL
Suitable occasion	Large conference	Smaller conference or group where you don't know the audience	Smallish group, probably internal, but not all known to you	Small team meeting where you know the other participants
Purpose	Provide information to many people	Provide information, but also get reaction	Provide information, hear reaction, respond; possibly discuss	Provide information, generate discussion
Stand or sit?	Stand	Stand	Stand or sit	Probably sit
Present from where?	A lectern	The front of the room	Either within the group or from the front	Your place at a table, or within the group
Visual aids	Yes, slides controlled from the lectern; can also use video or other multimedia	Yes, slides, but kept simple	Yes, but keep them to a minimum	Perhaps a one-page summary of your key points
Sound systems/ microphone	Yes	Yes	Probably not	No
Type of room	Large conference hall	Conference room or meeting room	Meeting room or office	Meeting room or office
Audience interaction	A formal question session afterwards may be usual	Formal questions, but you may get interruptions during your presentation	Fairly interactive; up to you to handle questions or discussion during the session	Likely to be very interactive if you allow

PART 2

Building Your Presentation

"All speaking is public speaking, whether it's to one person or a thousand."

—Roger Love

W hat if you've been asked to present a topic, introduce someone, or publicly share an experience, and it doesn't go well? Perhaps you decided to wing it without any preparation and spewed out a bunch of convoluted words and sentences that seemed to diverge in several directions during your speech. You delivered your message, but not as you would have preferred. A well-organized speech can make all the difference in the success of the presentation. An unorganized speech may leave an audience confused and the presenter disappointed.

Good organization is the key to an effective presentation because it helps clarify your message, making it easier to understand and easier for you to deliver and stay on point. Having a logical base to build on also makes it easier for you to develop your message.

CHAPTER 6

Preparing an Outline

A well-organized speech will
be easier for your audience to
follow and understand.

Writing guides will tell you that a story should have three parts: a beginning, a middle, and an end. The beginning is where the writer captures the audience's attention, sets the mood for the reader, and entices the reader to read more. The middle is where the bulk of the story resides, communicating important details while still holding the reader's attention. The end of the story closes with a conclusion and possibly offers a solution to a problem. A good ending leaves the reader satisfied and keeps them thinking about the story, even long after it's finished.

Good presentations also have a beginning, middle, and end, with the same audience benefits applicable to written stories. This structure can be applied by creating an outline. Outlining helps you develop a logical, clear message, making it easy to present in a way that the audience can understand. Without an outline, your message may lose logical integrity, with no apparent connection between points or relation to the topic.

A basic outline is a solid and useful way to organize your speech effectively. It consists of three parts:

1. Introduction
2. Body
3. Conclusion

This strategy has also been described as: "Tell them what you are going to tell them, tell them, then tell them what you told them."

PROCESS

To start, decide what you want to talk about. Select a theme or thesis for your speech. This is the main point you want to share. For example, your theme could be "Rooftop Gardens in San Diego: Why You Should Install One on Your Roof."

Next, complete an audience analysis (see Chapter 2, which describes this in more depth). This will help you decide how to best organize your speech. You may need to refine the topic to target your message to the needs of your audience.

Using the same rooftop garden subject, an audience analysis may show that most of your audience are not familiar with the topic or know very little about it. Let's say that the analysis also shows that most of the people who will attend your presentation live in Southern California, are between thirty and seventy years old, and are married. (Note: It may take some sleuthing to get audience details. See Chapter 2 for ideas.) You will want to tailor your presentation to this demographic.

Next, define the objective of your speech—determine your purpose for giving the speech and what you hope to achieve. Do you want to persuade, inform, demonstrate, introduce, or any combination of these? Also, think about what you want your audience to do with the information. Knowing this will help you determine the best organizational pattern for your speech.

🎤 TIP

Focus on one big idea. Don't try to tell too much. Avoid feeling as if you need to cram in a ton of information. You may confuse and bore your audience.

Continuing with the rooftop garden theme, let's say you're a rooftop garden installer. The *purpose* of your presentation is to increase awareness and interest in rooftop gardens. Your *objective* is to increase sales of rooftop garden installations.

After you've determined your main topic, you can then build subthemes or evidence to support and strengthen your theme.

For example, given what you know about your audience and to align with your purpose and objective, you might focus your speech on educating and building interest in the topic by highlighting the benefits of having a rooftop garden, such as increased privacy, improved carbon footprint, higher property value, and reduced energy costs.

Next, choose the best way to structure your outline. The following chart provides you with some ideas that can be used individually or in combination.

Presentation Structures

TYPE OF STRUCTURE	DESCRIPTION
Cause and Effect	This approach describes the cause first and then describes the result to help the audience understand the relationship between the two.
Comparison	The comparison method helps the audience understand how things compare, such as when comparing similar products or your product with the competition.
Problem and Solution	This approach works well when presented from the audience view (i.e., "Here is a solution to a problem you have"). You could start with a problem statement and then describe the ideal solution. The key for success with this strategy is convincing the audience that there really is a problem.
Spatial	Spatial patterns organize the speech according to how the topic exists in space. For example, if the topic of the speech is luxury yachts, the speaker will talk about each room on a yacht, perhaps beginning with those near the top of the boat and then working their way down by floor.
Time or Chronological	Chronological speeches are organized by time or sequence of events, using a beginning-to-end structure. For example, you may want to emphasize a change in something over time, such as the evolution of technology.
Advantage, Disadvantage, or Pro/Con	Use this approach to help your audience examine or understand issues, such as the advantages and disadvantages of regulating marijuana. Your purpose is to help the audience make their own decisions.
Comparative Advantage	Use this approach to show a comparison of similar or functional equivalent items and explain how one is more advantageous than the other.
Opinions	Speeches can also be organized by exploring different view-points. This format is often used for political topics or topics related to changes in the workplace.
Stories	Stories can be engaging and help to emphasize and explain a topic. For example, plots from literature, classic movies, and popular as well as real stories and life experiences can make for powerful narratives. Stories are typically structured with a beginning, middle, and end.

Continued

TYPE OF STRUCTURE	DESCRIPTION
Climatic	Climatic speeches are structured by order of importance, typically moving from the least to most important point.
Strategy Proposal	This approach is often used in business. Here is a possible outline: State the objective or purpose. • Describe the current conditions. • Describe the desired state. • List the possible strategies, with the pros and cons of each. • Address the budget if necessary. • Identify the best strategy and describe the next steps.
Project Update	This approach is often used in business. Here is a possible outline: Describe the project or provide a brief overview of it. Describe any critical outstanding problems. Describe how problems are being addressed. Describe successes to date and positive progress made. Close by listing the remaining steps needed to achieve the goals.
Persuasive or Promotion of a Product or Service	This approach is often used in business. Here is a possible outline: Frame the need that the product, service, or idea addresses. Describe the need in more detail. Describe the ways in which your solution addresses the need. Describe the benefits of the solution. Describe how the audience can act on the solution.
Facilitate Skill Learning	This approach is used to explain the value of a skill and show how it's done. Here is a possible outline: Frame the skill in terms of its importance to the audience. Explain the procedural steps involved. Get the audience to try some aspect of the skill or procedure or demonstrate how it's done. Review and summarize, including anything the audience didn't try or consider. Describe how the audience can apply the skill.
Presenting Bad News	This method is used to break bad news to your audience. Here is a possible outline: Explain the bad news. Describe what's been done to fix or resolve the situation. Explain what will be done to prevent it from happening again. Conclude with a call to action for the parties responsible for ensuring the fix.

WHICH STRUCTURE SHOULD YOU USE?

The structure you use for your presentation depends on the nature of your talk. Whichever structure you use should flow logically, expanding each point as needed with supporting evidence for argument, analysis, and appeal. For example, if you want to persuade your audience, consider addressing potential objectives and alternatives to showcase a reasoned, balanced view.

After you've determined the purpose, topic, and audience and selected the best organizational pattern for your speech, you're ready to prepare your outline.

Your outline should follow the structure you selected. Following are sample templates for your outline. Please notice that the templates are organized by separating the speech into introduction, body, and conclusion.

Sample speech outline: generic template

Introduction

- Greeting
- Attention-getting opening
- Topic (of your speech)
- You or your company's credibility
- Summative overview
- Benefits to the audience or others

Body

- Transition (signals moving from the introduction to the body)
- Main idea #1
  Supporting ideas
  Details/examples
  Visual/props (if applicable)
- Transition (signals moving from the one main idea to the next)

- Main idea #2
  Supporting ideas
  Details/examples
  Visual/props (if applicable)

- Transition (signals moving from the second main idea to the next)

- Main idea #3
  Supporting ideas
  Details/examples
  Visual/props (if applicable)

- Transition (signals moving from the body to the conclusion)

Conclusion

- Summary of main points (1, 2, and 3)

- Restatement of thesis

- Restatement of benefits

- Closer, clincher, and call to action

Sample speech outline: business proposal to investors template

Opening

- Attention-getting statement (i.e., "Invest $____ for ____percentage of the shares")

- Story to illustrate the need for the product XYZ

- Story to describe the vision of how product XYZ improves lives

Body: demo of product XYZ

- Benefits (focus on benefits, not features)
  Benefit #1
  Benefit #2
  Benefit #3

- Strength of the team

- Market analysis
- Financial projections

Conclusion

- Repeat call to action: "Invest $____ for ____percentage of the shares"

Sample speech outline: story-based template

- Attention-grabbing opening, which introduces the topic and core message
- Tell a story
    Make a point
- Tell another story
    Make *another* point
- Tell another story
    Make *another* point
- Memorable conclusion that ties together all three stories to support the core message

Sample speech outline: community or neighborhood association meeting template

- Story to introduce the problem (i.e., vandalism)
- Use facts and evidence to trace back to the core problem (i.e., lack of "safe" activities for youth)
    Statistics
    Reports
    Interviews
- Suggest a solution
    Budget
    Volunteers
    Stakeholders
- A strong call to action motivating the audience to join the cause

CHAPTER 7

Building Your Introduction

Tell us what you are going to tell us.

The purpose of the introduction is to gain audience attention and interest so they'll want to listen further. It's an important part of the speech because it sets the tone and can make the difference in how well you captivate your audience. If you don't get their attention and interest immediately, it can be difficult to do so as you continue with your presentation.

The introduction should include and address the following primary areas.

OPENING

Consider how you'll open your presentation. Will it include introducing other presenters? Will you greet your audience by saying something such as "Members of the Board," or "Good morning"? How will you get their attention and inspire them to continue listening?

You could begin with a startling fact, a story, or a question. The opening should relate to your topic and the audience. See Chapter 11 for additional opening techniques.

PURPOSE

Tell the audience the purpose of your speech and what you'll be speaking about. Avoid using jargon, and emphasize how the audience will benefit from what you have to share. Here are some examples:

"You'll learn how to . . ."

"I'm going to address . . ."

"I'm excited/pleased/honored to illustrate/explain/give you essential information about . . ."

CREDIBILITY

Share with the audience any pertinent information about you—and your organization, if applicable. This could include your qualifications, work experience, education, and awards that relate to the topic. You want to establish your expertise, credibility, and your right to speak on the topic. You could also address strengths about your organization, including number of years in business, growth statistics, and awards.

SUMMATIVE OVERVIEW

The introduction should also briefly outline the main points that you will address during the body of the speech. For example:

"First, we'll address the materials you'll need to . . .

Then, I'll explain the steps required to install . . .

Next, I'll show you . . .

And in the last part, you'll see a practical example of . . ."

BENEFIT

Make sure you let the audience know how they'll benefit from your speech—why should they care? What's in it for them? They can quickly disengage (and they might not stay) if they don't understand the value of the information. You can tie this part to a description of your purpose (why you're going to speak about the topic). It's vitally important to let the audience know how your presentation will benefit them from the onset.

LENGTH

You might let the audience know the approximate length of the speech to better maintain their attention. (I have found that people are less likely to get agitated if they know ahead of time how long a presentation will last.) You don't want your audience to constantly be checking their watches, wondering when you will be finished.

ACKNOWLEDGMENTS

If applicable, you may want to give acknowledgments, especially if you or your organization has been sponsored, supported, or encouraged by others, or if your work was a collaborative effort.

QUESTIONS AND RULES

Let the audience know at the beginning how you'll address questions (such as if and when you'll allow time for questions) and any other "rules" (such as silencing cell phones or refraining from eating) that apply to your presentation.

YOUR TASK

Go back to your initial outline and fill in the details about your opening. Here's a template/worksheet for the opening. Fill in details of what you'll say.

Introduction Worksheet

CRITERIA	NOTES
Audience greeting	
Attention-getting opening	
Preview of the presentation	
Clear objective or purpose	
Description of you/your company (establish credibility)	
State audience benefits	
Summative overview (what you'll talk about)	
Definition of key terms necessary for the audience to understand	
Length and acknowledgments	
Overview of any rules (i.e., handling questions, breaks, etc.)	

CHAPTER 8

CHAPTER 8

Building the Body of Your Speech

Tell us.

The middle, or body, of your speech addresses the content and information related to your purpose. It explains the key points you want your audience to know. The body is also the biggest part of your speech and takes up the most time relative to the opening and closing. If you've opened well, your audience will eagerly anticipate the details you present in the body.

Typically, the body consists of three major parts: main points, subpoints, and supporting details, including examples, arguments, facts, statistics, and stories as shown in the following body outline template. This is where your organizational patterns and structures apply (i.e., chronological order, cause and effect, problem and solution). See Chapter 6 for ways to organize a speech.

BODY OUTLINE

The body should be logically organized so it ties thoughts together uniformly, with points that support your main or key points and subsequent points building on the previous ones. This will help your audience follow along and help you remember the key point you want to address so you don't have to rely on notes. That structure should look something like this:

- Main Point 1
    Sub-points
    Supporting ideas
    Details and examples
    Transition . . .

- Main Point 2
    Sub-points
    Supporting ideas
    Details and examples
    Transition . . .

- Main Point 3
    Sub-points
    Supporting ideas
    Details and examples
    Transition . . .

Avoid addressing countless points that could become clouded with too many details and confuse and overwhelm your audience. Two to five main points is ideal for a speech of up to fifteen minutes long. If you have only one point in your speech, it will either be too short, or it will be too complex for the audience to follow. If you have one long point in your speech, you'll need to break that point into multiple sub-points. Five or more points should be reserved for longer public speaking engagements or more technical topics.

Most listeners remember very little of what they hear. Three seems to be the magic number of points for a fifteen-minute speech that the audience is best able to follow and remember.

Address enough key points relative to the length of the speech as shown here:

LENGTH OF SPEECH	NUMBER OF KEY OR MAIN POINTS
Ten- to fifteen-minute speech	Two to four key points
Thirty-minute speech	Five to six key points
Forty-five minutes to two-hour speech	Eight to ten key points

FILL IN THE DETAILS

As you begin to further flesh out your speech, consider including supporting materials to back your claims, such as examples, statistics, testimonies, or a narrative. These will add credibility to your speech.

Make sure you keep your message simple and to the point. Avoid overloading your audience with irrelevant and boring facts. Studies have shown that people typically remember only three facts from a presentation just ten minutes after it's over. Your audience may only want to hear what the issue is and how to solve it, so keep this in mind as your fill in the details.

Your task

Go back to your initial outline and fill in the details about the body of your speech (see the following template/worksheet).

Body Worksheet

CRITERIA	NOTES/DETAILS
Main Point #1	
Supporting point #1	
Details	
Supporting point #2	
Details	
Supporting point #3	
Details	
Main Point #2	
Supporting point #1	
Details	
Supporting point #2	
Details	
Supporting point #3	
Details	
Main Point #3	
Supporting point #1	
Details	
Supporting point #2	
Details	
Supporting point #3	
Details	

CHAPTER 9

Building Your Closing

Tell us what you told us.

Of course, if you "tell us what you told us," literally, your ending could be quite long and boring. Your speech ending should not be anticlimactic. If you've done a great job at engaging your audience throughout the speech, they'll be excited to learn what they can do with the information and how they can learn even more.

The closing provides an opportunity for you to help your audience understand why they listened to your presentation. It also can help you achieve your purpose, such as getting people to buy your books, purchase your products and services, convince them to take action, or change their beliefs. The summary, then, is just as important as the opening, because unlike the opening when it's necessary to grab your audience's attention, the summary can influence what your audience thinks about and whether and how they act on the information in your speech.

The end of your speech should summarize the purpose of your

presentation, with clear instructions on what the audience can do with the information and how they can benefit from it. For example, if you gave a speech about teaching your audience how to build an iPhone app, your summary could then briefly review the steps and showcase examples of the completed app and what the audience can do with the app (i.e., how they benefit).

The closing can include these points:

- A summary of the key points, highlighting the main ideas addressed in your speech
- A restatement of your purpose, reinforcing your message
- A restatement of audience benefits, reminding the audience of how they'll benefit from your message

INCLUDE A CALL TO ACTION

Consider what you want your audience to feel, think, and do with the information you provide. Ideally, your speech will leave a lasting, positive impression on your audience, and they will leave feeling enthusiastic, informed, and motivated to act. Clearly state what your audience can do with the information and how and where they can learn more about your topic. For example, you could:

- Share your contact information or pass out business cards and promotional materials.
- Include incentives such as free passes, trial offers, or discount cards.
- Make statements such as, "To take advantage of X, Y, and Z, come talk to me after this presentation," or "For more information, follow me on [social media site] and check out my website."
- End with a challenge, such as announcing an award to whomever sells the most product or service within a specific date following the presentation.

END WITH A STRONG FINAL STATEMENT

Your summary should also include a final statement that leaves a lasting impression. It should be clear to the audience that your presentation is finished. Here you can provide further consideration for your listeners. For example, you could end with a powerful and inspiring quotation relevant to your speech. This is also usually the time to ask the audience whether they have any questions.

Consider also ending your speech with positive thoughts. For example, you could end by stating good wishes to the audience, something about enjoying the rest of the day or evening.

And, of course, you should always thank your audience for their participation and attendance. Let them know you appreciate them taking the time out of their busy schedules to listen to what you have to say.

To determine how to end your speech effectively, consider what you want your audience to do, feel, and believe by listening to your speech. Do you want them to support, donate, or volunteer to a cause you're promoting? Do you want them to buy any products or services? Do you want them to change their beliefs and opinions about a cause, person, or organization? Do you want to inspire them to improve their confidence? Knowing your purpose can help you know what to ask for in your call to action and any relevant final statements.

There are several mistakes that you want to avoid when you end your speech. This includes ending your presentation abruptly, without any conclusion. Don't end your speech by suddenly stating, "That's all," without any kind of clear conclusion, leaving your audience potentially confused. Instead, give your speech closure. Prepare your audience for the ending by using transitional words such as, "As shown, you'll have a beautiful planter by following these simple steps."

You also want to avoid ending your presentation with an apology. Don't give your audience a reason to judge or question the credibility of the material or you. You don't want to end on a negative note.

And avoid ending with new material. This can confuse your audience and make it appear as if you're unorganized. The closing of your speech should be a recap of what they've already heard. This is your opportunity to reinforce important points you want them to remember later.

Now, go back to your initial outline and fill in the details about the closing of your speech.

Closing Worksheet

CRITERIA	NOTES/DETAILS
Summary of main points (1, 2, and 3)	
Restatement of your purpose	
Restatement of the benefits	
Call to action	
Closing statement	

Now you're ready to put together your entire outline. The following is a generic template of all three parts.

Entire Speech Outline Template
Worksheet Introduction

CRITERIA	NOTES/TASKS
Audience greeting	
Attention-getting opening	
Preview of the presentation	
Clear objective or purpose	
Description of you/your company (establish credibility)	
State audience benefits	
Summative overview (what you'll talk about)	
Definition of key terms necessary for the audience to understand	
Length and acknowledgments	
Overview of any "rules" (i.e., handling questions, breaks, etc.)	

Body

CRITERIA	NOTES/DETAILS
Main Point #1	
Supporting point #1	
Details	
Supporting point #2	
Details	
Supporting point #3	
Details	
Main Point #2	
Supporting point #1	
Details	
Supporting point #2	
Details	
Supporting point #3	
Details	
Main Point #3	
Supporting point #1	
Details	
Supporting point #2	
Details	
Supporting point #3	
Details	

Conclusion

CRITERIA	NOTES/DETAILS
Summary of main points (1, 2, and 3)	
Restatement of your purpose	
Restatement of the benefits	
Call to action	
Closing statement	

PART 3

Fine-Tuning Your Presentation

Sandpaper feels rough, but when
applied repeatedly, it creates a
smooth, pleasing surface.

A solid outline provides a foundation you can then use to expand and refine your speech. You must take that structure and build an engaging speech around it. After completing the outline, you should then come up with methods to present your ideas clearly and make crucial points in impactful ways. Your message should flow seamlessly, using language that resonates with your audience. Start your speech strong, and when needed, make it eye-catching, interesting, and engaging through the use of visual aids.

Your message should meet the expectations of the event, whether it is to inform, persuade, motivate, or challenge. Keep in mind that you are writing a speech for an audience, not an essay. It should be entertaining and capture interest. It should sound natural and authentic and be believable. People will most likely hear and not read your speech. Therefore, make your speech easy to understand and follow. This can be done through thoughtful wording and the proper use of transitions.

How you open your speech also matters. Lackluster, inappropriate, and confusing openings likely won't go over well with your audience. Do you ever watch movie trailers to determine whether the movie might be worth watching? Within just a few minutes, you decide whether to give the movie a chance. The opening of a speech is like a movie trailer; if done well, the audience will want to learn more.

Your speech can also be strengthened by supporting it with credible information. However, just throwing out a bunch of statistics and research results may not be enough. If done poorly, citing research can leave your audience frustrated and confused. However, if done well, providing statistics can make a big difference on the impact of your message, helping drive key points and emphasizing important information. You'll want people to believe what you are talking about. Adding in a few credible facts will help back up your statements.

Incorporating visuals into your speech can also make it more powerful. The audience usually will only remember a fraction of what you say. Slides and props can help the audience understand and remember your message, and they can be entertaining.

After completing your outline, these are elements that should all be considered when fine-tuning your speech.

CHAPTER 10

Writing Techniques to Refine and Polish

A good speech is written from the audience's view with three objectives: to impress, to elicit action, and to entertain.

Unless you're an accomplished public speaker, it's often best to write your speech before the event. Consider these techniques to refine and polish your speech.

VERBAL SIGNPOSTS

Your speech should flow well and be easy for your audience to follow. When writing your script, use transitional wording or verbal signposts between each of your main ideas to provide a pathway and direction of what you'll say. Just as road signs assist drivers with directions, verbal punctuation (indicating when you've finished one point and are moving on to the next) also assist listeners in following along with you. This can sometimes be done effectively with just a pause or change in pitch. It can also be clearly stated, such as when summarizing, "As you can see, we've explored key factors for . . ." or for a preview, such as, "We just learned how to set up . . . now we'll address how to use . . ." or "Now that we've seen . . . let's turn to . . ."

Use verbal signposts to also signal the end of your speech. Here are sample transitional phrases.

"As we've reviewed today . . ."

"Now you know the steps involved in building a . . ."

"As a result, I/we suggest . . ."

"I/We propose to . . ."

"My final comments address . . ."

Need more? Here's a list of possible transitional phrases.

EXAMPLES	SUMMARIZING	EMPHASIZING	REFERENCING PAST/FUTURE
• Now, let's take an example • To illustrate • For example • For instance	• To summarize • To sum up • Let me summarize by saying • In conclusion • In short • To recap what we've addressed so far	• What's important to remember is • I'd like to emphasize the fact that • This is very significant because • We need to focus on	• As we saw in part/step 1 • We'll go into more detail on that later • This will be the subject of part 3

> ### ① TIP
>
> Keep in mind that a good speech is written from the audience's, not the speaker's, point of view. Ideally, the audience will feel as if the message is intended only for them. They'll want to listen to you and forget that their chair is too hard, that they're hungry, or that they have other things to do.

As your write your speech, also think about how it will affect a greater audience and what message you want to convey to them. Steve Jobs's key messages, for example, were not just for the audience at the conference but for the entire world.

A strong speech also connects to your audience's hearts.

ADDITIONAL WRITING TECHNIQUES

Some of the most notable speech writers, coaches, and instructors suggest similar techniques for writing powerful, successful speeches. Here's a list of these common tips.

Powerful Speech Writing Techniques

CRITERIA	DESCRIPTION
Use only a few key points	Don't include too much, especially beyond what supports your topic. People typically may only remember just a few things.
No lengthy introductions and formalities	Keep the formalities short and sweet. By the time you're finished acknowledging and thanking everyone, you've lost your audience. Go right to the issue, and your audience will pay attention.
Keep it clear and simple	A clear and concise speech will be easier for your audience to understand and follow. Avoid unnecessary and vague words.
Get the facts	You want people to believe that you know what you're talking about. Support your statements with credible facts and statistics.
Use imagery	Create a picture in people's minds through vivid words related to your central theme.
Write like you talk	You're writing a speech, not an essay. People will hear the speech, not read it. The message should feel comfortable, more like an engaging conversation.
Use concrete words and examples	Concrete details keep people interested. For instance, a vague sentence such as "There must be less crime in our neighborhood" is much less effective than the more concrete "Let's implement a neighborhood watch program to educate residents of our community on security and safety; that way, when criminal activity is suspected, neighbors are encouraged to report it to authorities and not intervene."
Review and revise . . . several times	Don't take a "one and done" approach. Critically review your speech and cut out unnecessary information and wording. Revise as needed to ensure it flows smoothly, supports your topic, and is easy to understand.
End strong	End with a line people will remember that contains the message you want them to recall.

CHAPTER 11

Opening Strategies

What makes a great opening?

Communication advice from instruction guides, books, coaches, and educators says that one of the biggest keys to successful communication is to engage your audience. This applies to all channels of communication including emails, billboards, websites, social media, webcasts, flyers, reports, and, of course, presentations. As described in the case study that follows, communication is ineffective if it doesn't pique the interest and attention of the receiver and sustain it.

CASE STUDY: Lengthy Opening

John, a busy senior executive in a technology company, had a busy morning with back-to-back meetings scheduled before and

Continued

after a mid-morning industry webinar. The webinar moderator began the introduction with an irrelevant lecture about the state of the economy using clichés and generic statements and then continued with a lengthy introduction of each of the many guest speakers. The moderator then proceeded to thank several people who were involved in organizing the webinar. All of this took fifteen minutes, and the purpose of the presentation had not yet been addressed. John's patience ran thin, as he didn't have the time (or patience) to continue, so he left the webinar.

It's critical that the audience is engaged from the get-go. Think about how many emails and letters you've discarded because you lost interest after the first line of text. People are inundated with information and often quickly filter out what they deem as unimportant, making it difficult for messages to get noticed. This also applies to public speaking or any live presentation. An audience will quickly make value judgments about the presenter—including the topic and organization represented—during the first several seconds of the presentation. That initial judgment can stick, and once that judgment is there, it can be hard to change.

An effective opening sets the tone for the entire presentation. Ideally, you'll want to engage your audience at the beginning, having them at the edge of their seats in anticipation of what's to come.

During a June 2012 TED Talk, Jane McGonigal opened her speech with this statement: "You will live 7.5 minutes longer than you would have otherwise, just because you watched this talk."[2] Jane's

---

2   McGonigal, Jane, "The Game That Can Give You Ten Extra Years of Life," June 2012, TEDGlobal 2012, https://www.ted.com/talks/jane_mcgonigal_the _game_that_can_give_you_10_extra_years_of_life?language=en#t-35229.

presentation was filmed, and the camera picked up on the audience's reaction to her comment. Their faces appeared curious, and all eyes were upon her. She clearly had their attention, and they appeared excited and ready for more information. She then supported her statement with, "I have math to prove this is possible"—an effective lead-in to the topic of her speech. Her approach was effective.

START WITH A HOOK

Consider starting your presentation with a hook, something that gets your audience's attention immediately. A hook should be appropriate to your audience and relate to the speech, or at least be an effective lead-in to your speech.

Several years ago, I attended an all-day seminar facilitated by several speakers. It was an active morning with various workshops. Just after the lunch break, people filtered back into the auditorium, and the room became quite noisy as people conversed with those sitting next to them. As this was all happening, the scheduled presenter entered the stage from the side and walked very slowly, keeping his hands clasped in front of him and his head bent down, his eyes following his footsteps, to the center of the platform.

Some people noticed, while others continued to engage in their conversations. When the speaker got to the center of the stage, he stopped, turned toward the audience, but remained in the same position, with his head lowered and his hands clasped. He held that position for a few minutes without saying a word or making any noise. The audience started to quiet down, and more people focused their attention on him. After a few minutes in this position, he then raised his head, unclasped his hands, and just stared at the audience, moving his eyes back and forth across the room. He still hadn't said a word. He kept doing this until eventually the entire room quieted and all eyes were focused on him. It took about five minutes for him to engage the entire audience. Then, with a smile, he said, "Now that I have your attention, let's begin."

TIP

Praise your audience. Tell them how good they are. For example, you could state, "As experts in this field, you can understand . . ." or "Like you, people in the top 10 percent . . ." People like this, and they'll most likely feel happy and engaged.

The above method of silence worked. However, attention-getting hooks come in many forms. Select the most appropriate method for your targeted audience, one that aligns with your purpose. For instance, starting your speech with humor for a serious audience who might be skeptical of your topic may not be well received. In this case, a shocking valid statistic might be more appropriate.

MAKE IT INTERESTING

So how do you begin a presentation in a way that engages the audience? Here's what doesn't work: an opening that's humdrum, monotonous, drab, lame, lifeless, dull, and commonplace. For example, the dreary "Today, I would like to talk about . . ." approach is boring.

The ideal openings resonate with your audience on an emotional and intellectual level. Following are several powerful methods, a collection from various sources that can be used to grab the attention of your audience. It's quite a list, and any will work given the right circumstances.

Opening Strategies to Engage Your Audience

OPENING STRATEGY	DESCRIPTION
Rhetorical Question	Start your speech with a rhetorical question, one that gets the audience thinking without requiring them to answer. Rhetorical questions can create a dramatic effect and make a point. For example, Simon Sinek starts one of his TED Talk presentations with: "How do you explain when things don't go as we assumed?"[3]
Startling Statement	Start your speech with a statement that surprises your audience. Startling statements usually are factual and support the point you'll make. You may need to research credible, strong facts. For example, a presentation about conservation can start with, "About 3.5 million tons of trash is floating in the middle of our ocean."
Story or Anecdote	Tell a story, either personal or from another source, that relates to the subject. Your story should be stimulating enough to captivate the audience visually and emotionally. A well-told story can be very effective. The former late Apple president, Steve Jobs, often used storytelling to engage his audience. He started his 2005 commencement address at Stanford University by stating, "Truth be told, I never graduated from college, and this is the closest I've ever gotten to a college graduation. Today, I want to tell you three stories from my life. That's it, no big deal—just three stories. The first story is about connecting the dots."[4]
Suspense and Surprise	Another way to effectively open your speech is to build suspense followed by a surprising end or contradictory statement. For example, "The loud crash woke me instantly. I could feel my hair stand on end. My heart was nearly beating out of my chest. I lay there frozen, too scared to move. And then, within seconds, I felt a thump on my bed. I opened my eyes to see my cat. It purred."
Quotation	Quotations provide an initial thought or theme leading into the speech. It should be relevant to your speech and should be a quote from someone your audience is familiar with, perhaps an expert in the field you are speaking about.

Continued

3   Simon Sinek, "How Great Leaders Inspire Action," TedxPuget Sound, https://www.ted.com/talks/simon_sinek_how_great_leaders_inspire_action/transcript?language=en#t-4716%20.

4   "Steve Jobs Stanford Commencement Speech, 2005," YouTube, March 6, 2006, https://www.youtube.com/watch?v=D1R-jKKp3NA.

OPENING STRATEGY	DESCRIPTION
Challenging Question	Thought-provoking, challenging questions instantly engage an audience, getting them to think. Note: If you ask for a show of hands regarding what's being asked, they may be more likely to participate.
Humor	Humor is instantly engaging. If you can get people laughing, they'll feel more comfortable, and you'll feel more confident.
Testimonial	Reliable testimonials can be an effective way of establishing credibility.
Music	Music can direct an audience's attention and create a desired tone if used appropriately. Remember to consider the type of music you will play and sound level. You want to pick something your audience will enjoy.
Action	Action, such as acrobats, dancing, or jumping on stage, creates a sense of movement and energy. Use it briefly so it doesn't distract from your message.
Props	Props such as gadgets, a funny hat, samples, food, or costumes can easily introduce your topic and engage an audience.
Audience Participation	Invite or ask for a volunteer to participate.
Occasion	Comment on the occasion, especially if it's sentimental, such as an anniversary, wedding, or birthday.
Previous Speaker	Pick up on something a previous speaker said or did, especially if that person was the president, chairman of the board, or well-known guest speaker. It shows respect, validates their speech, and can lend you more credibility.
Reference to Current Events	A current event, especially regarding a hot topic widely addressed in the news, is relatable and thus engaging.
Historical Reference	Start your speech by referencing a historical event. You could then segue into your speech, such as "On this day in history, August 3, 1492, Columbus set sail from Spain, discovering America just two months later. The launch of our XYZ Product two months ago has reaped . . ."
Picture or Photo	The right picture can instantly draw on people's emotions. It can also be used to enhance and help clarify a point you want to make. Make sure it's a high-quality image.
Video	Play a short video. Videos can evoke an emotional response and are an effective way to show movement and sound. Imagine showing a short video of a professional surfer riding an enormous wave as an introduction to a sales meeting on a new line of surfboards.

OPENING STRATEGY	DESCRIPTION
Describe a Problem	Everyone has problems, and our first instinct is to think about possible solutions. Addressing pain points is a great way to begin a speech.
Silence	Sometimes doing nothing is most effective. People are so used to noise, especially around others, that when there isn't any, it can elicit attention. The audience will want to know what will happen next.
Statistics and Data	Showcasing compelling data and statistics can prove a point.
Imagination	Use the words *imagine*, *think of*, and *close your eyes* to get your audience to engage by using their imaginations.
What if?	Ask "what if" questions to help people consider how something could be. For example, you could ask, "What if you had $100,000 more in your bank account today? What would you do with it?" as a lead-in to a speech about money management.
A Promise	Tell the audience how they'll benefit by listening to your speech by saying something like, "By the end of this presentation, you'll . . ."
Arouse Curiosity	Like storytelling, a descriptive narrative designed to arouse curiosity can be an effective way to get your audience's attention. It could be self-deprecating humor, such as this opening statement about a speech on healthy eating: "Let me tell you something I admit I'm a bit ashamed of, probably even more embarrassed about. I had a moment of insanity and went for the jelly donut this morning. Oh. It tasted *sooo* good!"

CHAPTER 12

Emphasizing Audience Benefits to Captivate and Inspire

It's all about them, not me.

The best oral communication, regardless of the method, targets the listener effectively. Public speaking has the same goal. Your audience will more likely want to listen to your presentation if they understand how the message benefits them.

If you can show your audience how you're going to save them frustration, solve their problems, give them something, make them money, help them meet their goals, or understand their feelings, you have the makings of a powerful message.

Your audience will want to know "What's in it for me?" and "Why should I care?" Your message should clearly address audience benefits at the beginning. If the audience benefits are clear up front, your audience will more likely focus on the presentation for more information.

To effectively target your audience, emphasize the benefits you are providing. Use language such as "This presentation will teach you how to easily sell yourself to a potential employer" or "By listening to this presentation, you'll learn how to write winning proposals."

(🎤) TIP

Don't try to impress the audience by proving that you're smart; this can create distance between them and you. Instead, just be you— be real. You'll feel more connected to your audience and become approachable to them.

Let's say you're speaking to employees about implementing changes with how customer complaints are handled. If you merely describe the changes with instructions for implementation, you may be received with resistance if the audience doesn't understand why they should invest time and energy into the change. However, you're more likely to make your message impactful if you emphasize how they'll benefit by it. For example, you could say, "To meet customer expectations and build customer loyalty, improving these areas is key to generating and enhancing revenues and profits. The new customer resolution program links customer satisfaction to employee rewards, including quarterly bonuses based on a percentage increase in revenue." This way, the audience gets a clear idea of exactly what you're offering them.

USE VISUALS TO HIGHLIGHT AUDIENCE BENEFITS

Telling your audience how they can benefit is just one way to capture the audience's interest. Visual aids also can be effectively used to emphasize audience benefits, as shown in the message below that combines the symbol of money "$$$" with the message "Achieve Wealth."

USE THE WORD *YOU*

Another strategy to target the audience and emphasize benefits is to use the word *you* more than first person *I*, *we*, or *us*. The statement "We're excited to offer you a new healthcare plan that we're confident you'll love" implies how the audience will benefit, but it's not necessarily clear who the message is about as the emphasis is on the word *we*.

An improved revision might state, "You're eligible to enroll in our new healthcare plan that provides you with the same benefits at a fraction of the cost." Simply changing the word *we* to *you* can make a difference in how well the message is received.

USE INCLUSIVE PRONOUNS

Use of inclusive pronouns such as *we*, *us*, and *our* also helps you bond with and engage the audience. Shel Leanne, author of *Say It Like Obama: The Power of Speaking with Purpose and Vision*, and Kristin Arnold, author of *Boring to Bravo*, suggest that inclusive pronouns create a feeling of belonging and being part of a team, making the audience feel included in your speech. "It helps to send the message that the speaker and those listening are on the same team, in the same boat, facing the same fate."[5] For example, the statement "You must resolve this issue" implies that the audience is solely responsible and on their own. However, stating, "We can resolve this issue" instead implies that the speaker will work with them to achieve the results.

COMPLIMENT YOUR AUDIENCE

Another way of spotlighting or highlighting audience benefits is through compliments. Using compliments increases an audience's receptiveness, establishes a positive mind-set, and grabs the audience's attention.

The goal is to flatter your audience with compliments and praise to encourage them to take further action. This works because compliments:

- Make you feel good—people are more likely to agree to something (such as listening to your pitch or presentation) when they feel content and happy

- Provide positive reinforcement—studies have shown they encourage further action

- Improve confidence—flattery can improve people's confidence, increasing their enthusiasm about the activity (i.e., your speech)

Here are a few examples:

"Congratulations on a successful quarter. Thanks to your perseverance and hard work, our sales increased by 30 percent last quarter."

"Your perseverance and strong determination have paid off. Our

---

5   Shel Leanne, *Say It Like Obama: The Power of Speaking with Purpose and Vision* (New York: McGraw Hill, 2008), 78.

customer satisfaction rates improved significantly over last year's performance . . ."

"Your prototypes are impressive. Initial testing showed a strong demand. Let's brainstorm possible applications."

Making sure your audience knows what benefits you are providing helps ensure that you have their full attention.

CHAPTER 13

Using Data Strategically

Avoid data overkill.

I magine this: You're attending a national sales meeting presentation loaded with visuals full of detailed charts, tables, and graphs. Fortunately the presenter carefully explains each one, because the purpose of the visuals is not clear to you without further explanation. Does this sound familiar? Conversely, have you ever attended a presentation where you remember how well the data shown visually helped you understand the message? Hopefully yes, although often visual aids are full of analytics that can do more harm than good.

Avoid the temptation to present too much data. You may have spent a lot of time collecting, analyzing, and reporting, and you're eager to share all the data to show how much work you've done. However, your presentation will be much better if you only share important, relevant information that's well presented. Too much data can ruin the effectiveness of your message if it results in a confused and disinterested audience.

Don't overdo it, but properly presented facts and figures can help support your message, providing evidence to back up your argument and helping reinforce statements.

The key to successfully using facts and figures in your speech is to make sure they support and enhance your message and are presented in a way that's easy for your audience to understand.

Here are examples of how data can strengthen your speech.

USE DATA TO STRENGTHEN A STORY

Don't just show the data; use it to help tell your story in a more meaningful way. Stories bring your audience in, engaging their attention and triggering their emotions. Adding relevant data to a story can strengthen it and might be the key that ignites your audience's interest in your topic.

> ### TIP
>
> Tell stories. People may more likely remember important facts when explained with a well-crafted, engaging story.

ESTABLISH A SETTING

Data helps clarify your message, showcasing any parameters about your topic. For example, if you want to persuade your audience to support a new housing development you're proposing to the city, sharing related data about the impact on the economy, transportation, services, and environment will answer questions people may have. Using data to establish a setting can be very effective in a presentation.

IDENTIFY THE KEY POINTS

Pull out only the most important data that supports your key points to use in your speech. Don't overwhelm your audience with *all* your data. The audience will more easily follow along and absorb the speech if it's well organized with a few, clear key points that support the topic.

DON'T RELY ON TEXT ALONE

Don't read the text on a slide, or even worse, display a slide that has too much text, especially if the audience must strain their eyes to read it. They'll lose interest quickly. Be able to relay the message you are presenting on a slide in your own words; this creates a more interesting presentation.

USE THE BEST VISUAL

Make sure you use a visual that best represents what you're emphasizing, whether it's a pie chart, graph, or some other type of illustration. For example, if you're comparing performance over time, such as in quarterly sales, then a line chart instead of a bar chart (both shown next) would be the better visual.

You should also make sure that your graph or chart is complete, visually appealing, easy to see, and quickly understood. All labels should be correct, well proportioned, and clear; colors should be effectively contrasted to show differences easily.

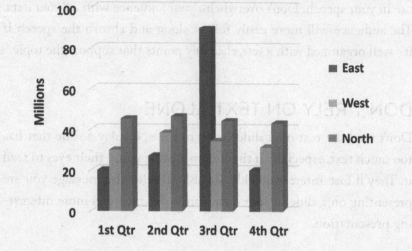

Good: Bar Chart

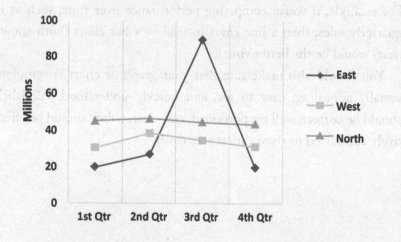

Better: Line Chart

KEEP IT CLEAR AND SIMPLE

It may be tempting to show everyone all your data so they can see how much work you've put into capturing it. Instead, only use a few key bits of information that clearly highlight your point. It's better not to show any slides than those that are too busy and confusing. Experts advise using only one to three data points per slide.

For example, which slide below do you think would be the easiest and fastest for an audience to see and understand?

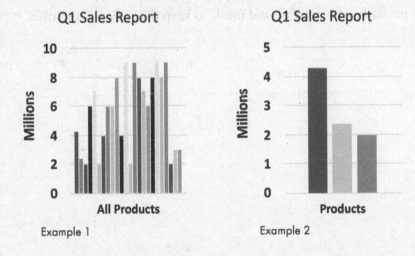

Example 1 includes too many products tightly clumped together, making it difficult for an audience to quickly understand. You could also consider grouping smaller products into three categories (see Example 2).

USE IMAGES

Consider using other images besides charts and graphs to drive home your message. Photos and illustrations can be a powerful method of evoking emotion and increasing an audience's emotional engagement in your message. It's also easier for people to process an image than it is to for them to assess charts and graphs.

MAKE IT FUN

Data doesn't have to be complex and boring. A good visual representation can be engaging and help the audience understand the information. Introduce some humor or present it in a way that's engaging and interesting, such as showing a video that creatively tells the story of your information. You could also apply humor to a story, possibly adding professional animation and music to keep the audience attentive.

CHAPTER 14

Using Visual
Aids Thoughtfully

Visual aids, used effectively, can strengthen
and enhance your speech.

The materials you use to strengthen your message comprise an important component of your presentation. Visual aids, such as slides, brochures, props, and videos, can do just that. They support and aid in the clarification and understanding of an oral presentation.

Studies have found that people remember just 20 percent of what they hear, 30 percent of what they see, 50 percent of what they hear and see, and 80 percent of what they hear, see, and do. Combining any of these activities can greatly increase comprehension and retention. Visual aids provide a powerful way of grabbing and keeping your audience's attention.

WHEN TO USE VISUAL AIDS

Use visual aids to help support, clarify, and maintain interest in your message. Effective visuals add impact and strengthen audience involvement.

Do not use visual aids if they're confusing, poorly designed and managed, or conflict with your speech; this can ruin your presentation. They should also not duplicate your speech, especially not word for word, and they should be designed such that an audience can easily see what they are and understand how they relate to what you are saying. When deciding whether to use visual aids, ask yourself these questions:

- Will visual aids enhance and help clarify my speech?
- Does the information need to be presented visually?
- Do I need to show information I can't easily say?

If you answered yes to these questions, then select visual aids that best support your speech; this might mean one type only, or something used in combination with others. There are many types of visual aids to choose from.

SLIDES

Slides, such as a PowerPoint presentation, are the most common type of aid used when presenting. They can be a powerful way to back up any presentation if they're not used as a crutch. In the early days of PowerPoint presentations, audiences could be easily distracted by type-writer text, obnoxious sound effects, and pointless, clunky, animated clip art. Fortunately, much of this noise is gone or has been upgraded to higher quality, more entertaining audio and video.

Visual aids, when not used correctly, can detract from the presentation. You may have heard the expression "death by PowerPoint." This sentiment represents the fact that the poor use of slides or poorly designed slides can detract from a speech. Frankly, they can ruin it.

Have you ever sat through a boring presentation where the speaker read each slide aloud, using them as their script, and thought, *I could have just read them myself at a much faster pace?* A presenter who is too reliant on their slides or overloads them with too much information will quickly frustrate and confuse the audience.

Instead, apply a "clarity by PowerPoint" strategy. Slides should be easy to see and understand. Avoid using too many words and content on each slide. The audience may focus on reading and understanding a slide that's too busy rather than listen to you. An illustration or a photograph may be all that's needed on a slide to best showcase your message. For example, imagine trying to explain the Matterhorn to someone who has never heard of it. Including a photograph with your explanation would be more effective than just an oral or written description (example shown below).

The Matterhorn is a mountain of the Alps, straddling the main watershed and border between Switzerland and Italy. It is a large, near-symmetrical pyramidal peak in the extended Monte Rosa area of the Pennine Alps, whose summit is 14,692 feet high, making it one of the highest summits in the Alps and Europe.

Here are additional ways to create clear slides that support and enhance your oral message.

- **Use colors and fonts that are easy to see.** Think "big"— big letters, big numbers, big everything. Colors should be high contrast. Colors that are too close might be difficult to differentiate. Bright colors are easier to see than pastels.

- **Consider your choice of colors** if there is a chance your audience has a color vision deficiency (CVD), which is the inability to see or distinguish certain shades of color. Most people with CVD have difficulty differentiating between red and green. A less common form of color deficiency is blue-yellow. People with CVD often see neutral or gray areas where a particular color should appear. In this case, consider using grayscale images instead of colors.

- **Keep your slides simple.** Use only a few words and pictures on each slide. A cluttered slide is distracting.

- **Use one idea per slide.** Each slide should support one point.

- **Display less than fifteen words per slide.** More than that may be hard for your audience to read, or they'll spend more time reading your slide than listening to you.

- **Make sure lists are aligned.** Use bullet points sparingly—about two to four bullet points maximum for each slide.

- **Keep slides unified.** Avoid slides that have too many inconsistent themes, designs, and style, which could be a distraction to your audience. Instead, consider using a master slide. You don't have to use the same ugly gray background, for example, for all slides. PowerPoint has many built-in default templates that can work well as a starting point and then be customized. PowerPoint isn't the only game in town, though; more slide creation options are available to provide a fresh approach to slide transition and layouts.

- **Make sure your slides don't have any grammar or spelling errors.** This distracts from your message and negatively affects your credibility.

- **Test your slides.** Colors seen on the computer screen may project differently on a large screen.

- **Avoid internet links in slides.** Unless you or your audience has an internet connection and the links work, consider downloading clips to your hard drive instead and embed them independently into your presentation.

- **Keep the content of each slide relevant to your speech.** If you are creating slides for online use and plan to use a voiceover, make sure that your spoken words apply to the words and images on each slide.

PRODUCT DEMOS AND PROPS

Product demonstrations and props (i.e., any physical objects) can be used to get your audience involved. They're especially useful when demonstrating the use of a company product. The presentation can be even more effective if the audience can touch, taste, and smell the product.

On the popular television reality show *Shark Tank*, entrepreneurs have only a short time to pitch their product or service to convince the panel of investors to accept and help fund their start-up. Contestants are advised to bring a prototype or props to enhance their chance at selling their idea. See Chapter 29 for more information about props.

HANDOUTS

Handouts can be an effective way for audience members to follow along. They can be used later as a reference for attendees, or they can provide additional information. You might hand out an outline of the presentation to help yourself stay on track. You can also use handouts to provide your contact information to the attendees.

However, handouts should not be given during a presentation unless they're used as a tool or part of the presentation, as they can be a distraction and interrupt the flow of information.

If you're planning to use handouts, make sure the design and quality is professional and consistent with the theme of your presentation. Here are some tips for producing high-quality handouts.

- Print your materials on heavy, high-quality stock (usually anything over 30 pounds and up to 80 pounds is used for brochures and flyers).

- Use semigloss instead of glossy paper. Glossy paper may be too reflective and can be hard to read.

- Make sure all images are clear.

- Use full-color printing for best effects.

- Use a professional printer for quality results.

WHITEBOARDS

Using a whiteboard is an effective method for presenting simple headings and illustrations and capturing comments from the audience, such as during a brainstorming session. A whiteboard also can be used as an interim method for presenting visuals when there is no access to technology and electrical power (although some whiteboards are electronic and interactive) or when the room is small with only a handful of attendees.

However, whiteboards can also detract from a presentation. You typically have to turn your back to the audience when writing on the board, which may make it difficult for your audience to hear you and see what you're doing. You'll also need to make sure your handwriting is legible and easily seen by your audience.

FLIP CHARTS

Visual Aids Checklist

Although rarely used anymore, flip charts can be an effective way to capture key information during a brainstorming session or capture responses from the audience. Flip charts are helpful to use when there isn't any access to technology or power source. Keep in mind that the handwritten information on flip charts can be illegible or difficult to read if poorly done. Writing on a flip chart also requires that the writer face the chart, instead of addressing and facing the audience directly. The action of flipping the pages can also be noisy and distracting. Flip charts don't work well when used in front of a large audience, as those sitting or standing in the back won't be able to easily see what's on the chart.

VIDEOS

Videos can be effectively used to engage an audience, demonstrate procedures, or show an action. They can trigger emotions as well, inciting your audience to act. You can also use videos as a part of a multimedia tool embedded in slides and various presentation software.

For on-site events, check that the location where you'll present has the technology and equipment available for showing videos, including a projector, screen, and internet connection.

Whichever visual aids you use, make sure they're indicative of what you're representing. There are positives and negatives for each method of presenting visually, so make sure you choose the right one for your audience, content, and venue. Remember, the quality of the materials can make or break the credibility of the speaker and organization.

Here's a checklist for reference when preparing your visual aids.

Visual Aids Checklist

CRITERIA	YES/NO
Slides are ready and in order.	
The visuals can be seen from all parts of the room.	
Visuals supplement and enhance the spoken message.	
Visuals are clear and don't display too much information.	
Visuals don't include any spelling or grammar errors.	
Visuals are appropriate for the message and audience.	
Referenced information is cited and sourced.	
The colors work well together. There's enough contrast that words and images are easily seen.	
I've practiced setting up and taking down visuals, so it's done smoothly during the speech.	
I've practiced maintaining eye contact with the audience while presenting the visuals.	
I've checked all equipment (overhead projector, computer, internet access, video, etc.) to make sure they work, and I know how to use them.	
I'm prepared to present without my visual aids in case I'm unable to use them.	
The picture resolution is high to avoid pixelation.	
There are no distracting sound effects or entrance/exit effects.	
I've practiced with my visual aids, so I know the timing of my speech.	
Visuals are used sparingly, not as a replacement for my oral speech.	
There's a consistent color scheme and format (titles, text, and background) throughout.	
Tables and charts are simple and easy to quickly understand.	

PART 4

Putting It All Together

"Take advantage of every opportunity to practice your communication skills, so that when important occasions arise, you will have the gift, the style, the sharpness, the clarity, and the emotions to affect other people."

—Jim Rohn

Putting It All Together

"Take care of your body. It's the only place you have to live."

—Jim Rohn

Perhaps you have a written script of your speech that you feel good about, and you already know the topic well and feel you have what you need to present. You may end up pulling off a great speech. However, a polished speech is likely the result of thorough preparation, beyond merely having a complete script. Most of what goes into the actual speech—the planning—is unseen by the audience. The time spent on the delivery is usually just a fraction of the time spent on the entire event leading up to it. What the audience should see is a speech delivered effortlessly. They don't need to know all the work you put into it behind the scenes.

Thorough preparation involves thorough practice. Just like learning to play an instrument or developing any new skill, practice is necessary to get better at something. Practicing a speech multiple times allows you to see how all the parts fit together and how you can refine it. Practice builds your confidence in the material and in yourself. The more comfortable you are with your delivery, the better your performance.

Thorough preparation also involves making sure that all of the t's are crossed and the i's are dotted—that all necessary factors, such as knowing the location of your speech, are addressed before the actual event. You'll want to make sure that your audience is comfortable when attending your presentation and that you have what you need (a microphone, lectern, and so on) for your delivery.

Considering the fine details pertinent to your speech will ensure that you have thought through every aspect of the speaking experience and prevent facing any surprises on the day of your presentation. It can also help you discover how you may enhance your speech. Whatever the presentation event, no matter how big or small, what is most important is that the presenter arrives prepared.

CHAPTER 15

Practice to Present Comfortably and Naturally

A well-polished speech will
be easier to deliver.

Many people have told me that they prefer not to practice their speech because they believe that if they memorize it, they'll end up sounding robotic. Some have also told me that practicing causes them to focus on their fear of public speaking. "I would rather not think about my speech beforehand so I don't build up any nerves," stated a student in one of my communication courses.

Using only an outline, without practice, may be acceptable for situations where you didn't have much time to prepare or are skilled at presenting. Maybe you've given the presentation before, so you think you don't need to prepare and can just go out there and kill it. And you *may* be able to effectively present without preparation, but . . . would you rather stumble during practice or in front of a live audience?

Practice as though it's the real thing. Practice at the venue where you plan to give your speech (or at some place that resembles it). You'll learn of any issues to address prior to your presentation, and you'll feel more comfortable when on stage for the actual presentation.

If you want to know how your presentation will go, do it in advance. Practice your speech in front of friends, colleagues, or family—or send them a recording of your speech. Ask them to be sincere and critical, and don't allow yourself to get your feelings hurt. It's better that you know of any areas where you can improve than deliver a poorly presented speech in front of a large audience.

Here are some very practical ideas for perfecting your presentation.

CONCEPTUALIZE

Envision the key points you want your audience to know. Think about how you'll transition between these key points. Conceptualizing helps you think through your material, and this is a form of practicing your speech.

SPEAK AUTHENTICALLY

Avoid speaking as if you're reading from a script. Instead, internalize the material and speak in a conversational tone, derived from being passionate about your topic.

PRACTICE OUT LOUD

Practice your speech out loud so you know how it feels and sounds and what your overall comfort level is. This can help you assess how well you speak and show you if there are any issues (speaking too fast or too slow, using filler words, poor articulation) that you can work on and avoid when speaking live in front of an audience.

PRACTICE STANDING (STRAIGHT) UP

Practice your presentation standing up, and envision yourself on stage in front of your audience. Stand tall—with your shoulders down and back, your back straight, and your head held high—and lean in slightly toward the audience. This posture not only makes you appear more confident and credible, it also helps you speak with more energy. Speaking hunched over or sitting can crowd your diaphragm, making it difficult to exhale enough air for powerful speaking.

RECORD YOURSELF ON VIDEO

Either record yourself or have someone else record you. Then upload and review the video to assess what you do well and identify areas to work on. Look for possible issues with movement and voice, such as nervous or distracting tics, use of fillers in your language (i.e., *uh* and *um*), unfamiliar or inappropriate wording, saying anything that's unclear, and doing or saying anything distracting that you weren't aware of (such as fidgeting unnecessarily). Note any areas for improvement that you can correct through more practice.

PRACTICE PRESENTING TO YOUR PET

If no one is available (or willing) to listen to and provide feedback about your speech, consider practicing in front of the next best thing . . . your pet. It may sound silly, but practicing your speech to a nonjudgmental animal, especially a dog, can be an effective means of "stepping out of yourself," allowing you to focus more on presenting (rather than how you feel). If you can get a pet's attention long enough, you may even smile through the process, helping you feel more relaxed overall.

MOVE AROUND

Practice the movements you'll use for your speech. The more you practice, the more likely you'll do the intended movements during your actual speech without having to think about them. For example, instead of standing "frozen" in one place on the stage, consider walking periodically across it so you can better address the entire audience. Practicing this beforehand will help you do it seamlessly and less awkwardly during your presentation. This also applies to hand gestures or any other movements. I doubt many readers would do a backflip on stage, but if that is part of your speech, you would not only want to know how to do one, but also what it feels like to do one in front of your audience.

PRESENT IN THE SAME CLOTHES

Practicing in the same clothes that you'll wear for the presentation can help you get a sense of how well the clothes fit and move with you and if they're too tight, scratchy, or otherwise a possible distraction. You definitely want to wear something that's comfortable and easy to move around in. And please consider the shoes you plan to wear. Are they comfortable? You want to make sure the bottom of the soles aren't slippery.

TIME IT

Determine how much time you want to spend on each section and each key point of your speech, and then time each one. You will want to spend approximately the same amount of time on each of the topics that you will cover. Also, time the entire speech so you have an idea if you need to revise, and where, to keep your speech within a specific time.

REHEARSE WITH VISUAL AIDS

Practice using your props and visual aids, including slides, handouts, and video, so you're comfortable using them. Always have a backup plan for delivering your presentation if the technology doesn't work. You never know what curveball you may get thrown when it's time to present, and it's best to be prepared for any situation.

PRACTICE WITHOUT NOTES

Practice without your notes, using them less and less with each practice until you can wean yourself off of them completely. Your goal should be to only use your notes if it's absolutely necessary to prompt you. Part of being prepared and able to give an engaging presentation is not having to rely on reading your notes.

LISTEN TO AN AUDIO RECORDING OF YOUR SPEECH

Record the audio of your speech and listen to it multiple times. Note what you did well and what you need to improve. Recording yourself helps you listen carefully for distracting speech patterns. For example, you might not know that you have an awkward laugh, or that you constantly end your sentences with an increasing pitch, even when you aren't asking a question. You might find out that you sniff or clear your throat a lot, or run sentences together without pausing, or speak too slowly or too quickly, softly, or loudly. These are things you can identify and then work on to improve.

VISUALIZE YOUR SUCCESS

Visualize being on the stage, presenting confidently to an engaged audience. Imagine that you are delivering a powerful speech that is well received by your audience. Envision them fully engaged and smiling throughout your delivery, finishing with a standing ovation at the end. The power of positive thinking is a wonderful thing. The more you visualize yourself being successful, the more it is likely to be a reality.

PRACTICE EYE CONTACT

Practice maintaining eye contact with an entire pretend audience (unless you have the benefit of practicing in front of a live audience). As you do this, avoid looking at anything else, such as your visuals or the back wall. You can do this at home, the office, or any setting. Pretend that you're standing in front of your audience using visuals or props as you practice your speech. You might even tape pictures of people's faces to chairs set up in front of you.

Look directly at each "face" for a few seconds (for about as long as it takes to say one sentence) and then move on to another face. Speak to all of the "faces," moving your direction across the entire "audience." You can also practice maintaining eye contact with the camera (i.e., on your computer or phone), which can represent the eyes of your audience.

TAKE A DEEP BREATH AND SMILE

Just before you begin speaking, calm yourself by standing straight, facing your audience, and taking a deep, silent breath—and then smile. This will relax you and help you breathe naturally so you'll be more likely to speak authentically.

Practicing will make you a more confident presenter. You'll feel more comfortable, and you'll present with ease, putting your audience at ease as well. They'll focus on the message and not on you.

Practicing also helps you build a strong command of your message so you can adapt it on the spot when necessary as you move along. Former president Bill Clinton, for instance, sometimes revised on the spot his well-rehearsed official speeches to match the mood of the moment.

Successful athletes, musicians, and artists spend endless hours rehearsing, analyzing, assessing, and working on their craft. Practice improves implementation. Steve Jobs was an outstanding speaker, and he thoroughly practiced his speeches over and over. He also required the same of outside speakers who presented at Apple. So practice. It will make your speech run better and more smoothly, and you will be prepared.

CHAPTER 16

Setting Up and Managing a Presentation Event

A well-polished speech is only as
good as how well it's managed.

With a little bit of planning and management, you'll be able
to deliver your speech effectively, without unnecessary
distractions and issues. This chapter contains guidelines
for ensuring the environment is well set up for your speech.

EQUIPMENT AND MATERIALS

If possible, get access to the room where you'll be presenting to check
that all the equipment—including your computer, or an on-site

computer, video equipment, and a projector—you'll need are working correctly and you know how to use them.

SEATING

Arrange the seating for optimal audience placement. If possible, visit the location in advance of your presentation, so you can access the seating options. Find out who will set up the layout and if you can arrange the seating just prior to your speech; then plan accordingly. Ideally, you'll want all attendees seated in a way that they can hear and see you. Consider the viewpoint from every seat. If you're using any kind of visuals, make sure every seat has full view of them.

If you find out in advance that you don't have control of how the seating is arranged, then you can at least revise your speech as needed to the fixed layout.

SOUND SYSTEMS AND MICROPHONES

If you're presenting in a large room, you'll likely need access to a sound system, including a microphone. Check these items before you present.

- **Check to see if the microphone you will be using is wireless or wired.** Wired means you'll be tethered, while wireless enables you to move around.

- **Know how to use the microphone.** A simple thing like knowing how to turn off and on the microphone may be easily missed. Find out how to do this *before* you start speaking so you don't accidentally start speaking into a microphone you didn't know was already on.

- **Plan to wear an outfit that can support a clip-on microphone.** A shirt with a pocket or collar works well. However, having a clip-on microphone attached to thin, sheer material won't look good, and it may not hold sufficiently. Make sure you don't wear anything that can bump against the microphone and be heard by your audience, such as long, dangling earrings.

- **Speak with your normal voice into the microphone.** Microphones amplify sound, so you don't need to shout or raise your voice. Instead speak as you would normally.

- **Don't magnify unpleasant sounds.** Be aware that the microphone not only picks up on all noise near it, it also magnifies it. Coughing, sneezing, or blowing your nose will be easily heard by your audience (and these are not pleasant sounds). Turn away from the microphone if you need to sneeze.

FINAL PREPARATION

Make sure you arrive at the venue with plenty of time before your speech. Don't arrive late or right before you're scheduled to present. Give yourself enough time to do last-minute checks and necessary setups as needed for seating arrangements, audio (check volume) and video equipment (make sure the video is set to the correct beginning), and the lectern and microphone. Allow yourself enough time to get a feel for the room, the size, the lighting, the temperature, and the overall setup. Also, take a few minutes before your presentation to review your notes and calm your nerves (deep breathing, meditation, or whatever works for you). You'll feel better prepared and less anxious.

DURING THE PRESENTATION

If you're introduced, remember to acknowledge that person, smiling and thanking them, and shaking their hand if appropriate. Acknowledge your audience as well. Address them warmly by smiling and maintain eye contact with them throughout your speech.

Delivery

"What you do speaks so loud that I
cannot hear what you say."

—Ralph Waldo Emerson

PART 5

Delivery

What you do... speaks so loud that
I cannot hear what you say.

—Ralph Waldo Emerson

ow you say your message is just as important as what you say. Your voice and nonverbal movements communicate and affect how the message is received. Can you imagine a comedian delivering a long list of jokes stone-faced, without ever cracking a smile or laughing? Not likely. Smiling and using your voice effectively can enhance your presentation. For example, varying your voice, speaking louder to emphasize key points, will get your message across more impactfully. Similarly, your nonverbal movements affect how a message is received. For example, stretching your arms out wide to demonstrate how big something is might be easier to understand than just stating it directly (i.e., "the device measured 4 feet long").

Words convey meaning. Nonverbal cues and vocal delivery can complement and accent your words, bringing life to them. However, these must be congruent with the words for the audience to understand the message. Otherwise, the audience might be confused or rely on what they are seeing and hearing rather than on what you are saying. You may have experienced this when someone says they are not upset, but the look on their face tells a different story.

CHAPTER 17

Mastering Your Voice

It's not what you say; it's how you say it.

W e've all felt tense listening to a presenter struggle, speaking too quickly or too slowly. Maybe they used too many fillers such as *um* and *uh*, or spoke in a boring, monotone voice that put you to sleep.

Voice distractions can, well . . . distract from the message, turning the audience's attention away from it. I've had students, bored with someone's lecture, tell me they counted the number of times the presenter said the word *um*. When asked what they got out of the presentation, their response was "Not to say *um* during a speech." That certainly is a takeaway, but probably not what the presenter intended.

If you're worried you might be "that" person who's not an adept speaker, or you just want to improve your presentation voice, you can! Habit-forming speech issues can be undone. Here are some guidelines to put you on the road to vocal finesse.

> ## ⓘ TIP
>
> The human voice can be made stronger with exercise and use. Practice speaking clearly and powerfully, carefully enunciating and putting energy into every word. You can do this any time.

FILLER WORDS

Many, if not most, people use filler words and phrases such as *um, uh, like, mm, actually, honestly, basically, you know,* and *I think that,* and most of them are not aware that they do this until someone else points it out to them. While challenging, it can be avoided. Here are some things you should keep in mind that will help you stop using filler words and improve your speech habits.

Assess how often you use filler words

Knowing how often you use filler words is an important first step in getting rid of them. This can be done by:

- Recruiting someone to track your fillers. Have them count the number of times you say fillers such as *um* or *uh.*

- Recording your voice. Use a digital voice recorder such as your cell phone and listen for any fillers used.

- Videotaping yourself. You'll be able to not only listen for any fillers, but also see the impact on facial and other expressions when you use fillers.

Understand why you say filler words

Assessing why you might be using filler words can give insight into how you might be able to avoid them. Filler words are commonly used when a speaker isn't prepared and doesn't know the information well. People struggling to know what to say will fill in that space with filler words. If the brain doesn't have words to pull from memory, it may create words on the fly (i.e., fillers).

Filler words aren't always bad. They can actually fulfill a purpose in certain contexts. For example, filler words used during a phone conversation can fill a void, inferring to the receiver that the other person is still on the line and thinking about something and not ready to turn back over the conversation. Without the filler words in this situation, the person on the other end may misinterpret the silence and take control of the conversation.

However, most of the time filler words are useless. When presenting in front of a large audience, for example, no one in the audience would consider the dead space as an opportunity to speak up.

TIP

Make sure you get adequate rest prior to your presentation. A well-rested brain is likely to be more alert and will reflect that in your voice and demeanor. You'll find it easier to articulate when you're alert than when you're tired and stumbling over your words.

Slow down

Speaking too quickly can make it difficult for your brain to keep up, causing you to add in meaningless filler words until you know what to say next. Instead, slowing down, even slightly, will help you articulate as you think about what you're saying. (But don't speak too slowly; this can be boring for your audience.)

Be realistic about how much time you have to present your material.

If you feel as though you have a limited time, you may speak faster than you would normally.

Pause with silence

Many communication experts advise replacing fillers with silence. I agree. I found this to be the best and easiest method of eliminating them, but it takes practice. It took me a good amount of time and effort to reduce the number of fillers I used and replace them with pauses instead. I had to consciously think about pausing between sentences, but over time it became easier.

In my profession, I frequently speak in front of an audience, so I've had lots of opportunity to practice this in real-world circumstances. However, you can use this method in almost any situation, such as when speaking conversationally with someone or practicing a mock presentation in front of a pretend audience. I recommend recording yourself so you can observe your progress.

Former president Barack Obama used pauses strategically to get the attention of his audience. He paused so the audience could process and consider his words.

Focus on your message and make eye contact

Avoid multitasking when it's important that you verbally communicate well. It becomes much more awkward to say "um" when making eye contact with your audience and when focusing on your words. Experiment with this at your next meeting or workshop. When on a phone call, for example, focus on your notes and what's being discussed. Don't look out the window, at your computer screen, or doodle. During a meeting, look at each person, giving them your full attention. You'll likely find that your use of filler words will lessen.

Plan your transitions

Not only will it make your speech flow more fluidly, transitional wording such as "Next we'll address" or "The next required step is" can help you avoid saying *um* and *uh*. Practice using transitional words and phrases until they become part of your vocabulary and are readily available to you as needed. Over time, you'll feel more inclined to use them, lessening your dependence on the fillers.

Monitor your progress

Periodically, monitor your progress. You may be surprised that with focused practice, you'll use those *uhs* and *ums* less.

VOLUME

You may have the best speech ever prepared, with targeted and engaging visuals and a captive audience. However, none of that matters if no one can hear you. The volume of your voice plays an important role in the success of your presentation. Research has shown that the quality of a person's voice affects how people perceive their credibility, confidence, and overall professionalism.[6]

So, what does that mean for you? How can you improve your volume and achieve a powerful voice?

The key to a powerful voice is to speak loud enough to be clearly heard. Research has shown that listeners associate variances in volume, such as louder tones, as representing authority.[7] Research has also

---

6   Kate Moran, "The Impact of Tone of Voice on Users' Brand Perception," Nielsen Norman Group, August 7, 2016, https://www.nngroup.com/articles/tone-voice-users/.
Preston Ni, "What Your Voice Reveals about You," Psychology Today, July 31, 2016, https://www.psychologytoday.com/us/blog/communication-success/201607/what-your-voice-reveals-about-you.

7   Sei Jin Ko, "The Sound of Status: People Know High-Power Voices When They Hear Them," Association for Psychological Science, November 24, 2014, https://www.science-daily.com/releases/2014/11/141124081040.htm.

shown that people in a position of power speak loudly, with high-er-pitched, monotonous voices.[8]

Raise your voice to the volume necessary for it to be heard by the people in the back row. In large rooms, or when using videoconferencing equipment, you may want to use a microphone.

BE HEARD: MINIMIZE NOISE

No matter how loudly you speak, any other noise besides your voice will be a distraction. It's therefore important to minimize these other noises. The following is a list of possible noise distractions you should be aware of and may need to address.

- **Noises coming from open windows and doors.** Make sure the windows and doors are shut to avoid noisy lawn mowers, traffic, kids playing, dogs barking, and vacuums.

- **Noises from you, other than your voice.** Avoid sounds you create that may be heard by your audience. Don't wear noisy jewelry (that a microphone can easily pick up and magnify) or hard heels that make a sound when you walk. Avoid making tapping noises with your fingers or nervously clicking a pen.

- **Noises from the audience.** If necessary, politely address the chatterers. It's disrespectful of them to not take your time and effort into consideration. The chatterers may otherwise be unaware of their effect without intervention.

- **Talking over audience chatter, laughter, or applause.** It's common for speakers to start speaking over the audience, including their applause, to quiet the room. It can work, but your

8   Sarah Griffiths, "The Sound of Status: Powerful People Develop Loud, High-Pitched, Monotonous Voices, Study Claims," Daily Mail, November 24, 2014, https://www.daily-mail.co.uk/sciencetech/article-2847208/The-sound-STATUS-Powerful-people-develop-loud-high-pitched-monotonous-voices-study-claims.html.

audience may not hear your first words. Instead, try motioning, waving your hand in a downward movement to indicate it's time to be quiet, or just wait for the applause to finish before you begin speaking.

You can also use your voice strategically to maximize your effectiveness by following these techniques:

- **Vary your volume.** Speaking at the same volume for any length of time can be monotonous and puts people to sleep.

- **Emphasize key words or phrases.** Speak slower, louder, or softer as appropriate.

- **Finish sentences strong.** Trailing off at the end of a sentence can not only make it difficult for your audience to hear, but it can also appear as if you're unsure about what you're saying.

PITCH

Pitch is basically the highs and lows of the speaker's voice. Pitch varies for men and women, reflecting differences in larynx size. Adult male voices are usually lower-pitched than female voices.

Pitch can help communicate emotions and affect the meaning of words, such as increasing your voice at the end of a question or to emphasize a specific word. For example, if you yell "ouch" in response to unexpectedly touching something hot, the pitch of your voice will likely be high.

Use some variation in pitch. Speaking at the same pitch for the entire presentation is monotonous to an audience, and you could lose their attention.

TONE

Tone is similar to pitch, with the emphasis on the emotional content carried by our voices. It's how words are spoken based on a person's emotions. For example, a person who speaks energetically can be considered as using an enthusiastic tone. A person who speaks with little effort in body movements, as well as minimal facial expression or variance in voice, can be considered to have a flat tone. You want to speak with a tone your audience will find engaging.

RATE

The term rate refers to speaking pace. The rate matters when speaking publicly. Speaking too slowly, too quickly, or at a constant clip without any variation can bore and frustrate the audience. Speak too quickly and you'll lose them; speak too slowly and you'll frustrate them. However, pausing between thoughts and sentences gives the audience time to process the information.

Ideally your voice should be clear, regardless of how fast you speak. Good enunciation and pronunciation will result in clear language more easily heard and received by an audience. Here are four factors to consider regarding the rate at which you speak.

Your normal speaking rate

This is the rate you're most comfortable using, which isn't necessarily good or bad. Some people talk fast, and some talk slowly. Your normal rate is influenced by many factors, including culture, family, geography, and profession.

Nervousness and stress

Speaking under pressure often makes you speak faster. If you're worried about speaking too quickly when presenting, consider writing the word slow or just the letter S (or whatever works for you) on your notes, finger, or someplace where you'll easily see it as a reminder to slow down.

Mental fatigue

People speak more slowly and with less articulation when they are tired. The solution is to get some rest prior to your speech (or at least take a break before your speech).

Complexity of content

It's common for people to describe complex information using longer words and sentences, causing them to pause more and speak more slowly. (Try speaking long, complex words quickly; it takes effort.) Slowing down helps an audience understand, and pauses also help them to process the information. Be careful about using uncommon words and phrases, especially if your audience might not easily understand them.

RESONANCE

A strong voice has good resonance. Resonance is the quality of the voice that makes it pleasant to listen to. Good resonance requires correct breathing and strong lungs. For good resonance, breathe in deeply, expanding your belly out as far as possible. Then tense the diaphragmatic muscles below your rib cage to hold the air. Release a little air out at a time as you speak, and you'll have good resonance. Practice this before your speech to become comfortable doing it so you don't focus on it and it doesn't appear obvious to your audience that you're doing this.

With proper breathing, your voice will stay strong and clear during your entire presentation.

CHAPTER 18

Key Body Language Techniques

Actions—your body movements—really
do speak louder than words.

once attended a lecture where the presenter constantly made a smacking sound with his lips, as if he were trying to clean peanut butter stuck to the roof of his mouth. The more he smacked, the more I focused on it, becoming unnerved and disinterested in his speech. I've also witnessed a presenter standing frozen in front of the room, expressionless and motionless, except for the movement of his lips. This was also very distracting.

Nonverbals, or your body movements, are just as important as your actual speech. Studies have shown that the words you use make up just a fraction of how communication is understood.[9]

Body language and tone are what primarily impact communication. Eye contact, body orientation, posture, facial expressions, and gestures affect how your audience perceives and understands your message.

> ## (!) TIP
>
> Smile! Unless you are delivering sobering news or when inappropriate, focus on smiling. People are more likely to receive information well from someone who is happy to deliver it.

Your body language is the external expression of what you feel and think inside. It rarely lies. Keep this in mind when presenting. If you're unenthusiastic about your topic, your body movements may also appear unenthusiastic, affecting your posture and voice. Your audience will pick up on this. It helps to be passionate about your topic.

However, you can also use movements to enhance your message and engage the audience. For example, you could use your fingers or hands to demonstrate the size of something. Movement requires energy, and energy is engaging. Instead of standing like a statue fixed in front of a lectern where people can't read your body language, consider using the whole stage as your platform, periodically walking to each side (while still facing the audience). Just don't pace back and forth like a caged panther.

---

9   Lucy Debenham, "Communication: What Percentage Is Body Language?" Body Language Expert, May 15, 2018, http://www.bodylanguageexpert.co.uk/communication-what-percentage-body-language.html.
     Albert Mehrabian, *Nonverbal Communication* (New Jersey: Aldine Transaction, 2007).

Be aware of your actions on stage and on camera. All actions and movement should reflect a positive demeanor and enhance and clarify your speech. You want to appear comfortable and relaxed.

EYE CONTACT

This counts as body language. Have you ever spoken to someone who looks right through you as if you don't exist, or continues to look the other way? You may quickly lose interest, respect, and patience with that person.

Yet many public speakers do the same thing. They present to an audience as if they don't exist. Perhaps they were following the common advice to look at the back of the room, just above people's heads. Have you heard that one before? While that can work to help calm fears, it will also annoy and quickly disengage an audience.

One of the primary rules of the nonprofit educational public speaking and communication organization Toastmasters is to "speak to people's eyes" in cultures where eye contact is valued such as in the United States. (Note: Some cultures may consider this activity as an invasion of privacy.) Looking people in the eye when in one-on-one situations tells them you're serious about what you're saying and focused on them. This applies when speaking to audiences as well.

Speakers make eye contact with their audience for a couple of reasons. First, it tells the audience that the presenter is honest. It creates a bond of trust. It also tells the audience that the presenter is confident in the material. The audience may interpret that to mean the presenter knows the material well. By maintaining eye contact, the audience will be more likely to remain engaged because they believe in the presenter.

Studies have found a connection between buyer behavior and eye contact on packaging.[10] Buyers are more likely to buy a product if the image (such as a person or animal) appears to be looking directly at them. A study presented in the journal *Environment and Behavior* found that consumers are more likely to purchase a cereal box if the cartoon characters shown on the box appear to make eye contact with them. According to the study, "[R]esearchers at Cornell University manipulated the gaze of the cartoon rabbit on Trix cereal boxes and found that adult consumers were more likely to choose Trix over competing brands if the rabbit was looking at them rather than away." These findings may also transfer over to speaking in public.

Scan the audience, making eye contact with as many people as possible. However don't lock eyes on one person. That will make the person, and possibly the rest of the audience, feel uncomfortable. It puts that person on the spot and causes the rest of the people to feel as if they're attending a private presentation to one person. When presenting in front of a camera, keep your eyes on the lens of the camera, unless you are being filmed having a conversation with others. (Then you would maintain eye contact with whomever you are talking to.)

HANDS

Hands can be important and useful tools for demonstrating an idea (such as gesturing the size of something). However, avoid flailing them about randomly, which can be distracting and annoying to the audience. Keep your arms and hands calmly at your side, and use them as needed. Don't fold your arms with your hands hidden in the folds at your chest, as this is considered defensive body language.

---

10   Mike Bartels, "How to Own Consumer Attention at Four Critical Touchpoints Using Eye Tracking," Tobii Pro (blog), https://www.tobiipro.com/blog/how-to-own-consumer-attention-4-touchpoints-eye-tracking/.
Jesper Clement, "Visual Influence on In-Store Buying Decision: An Eye-Track Experiment on the Visual Influence of Packaging Design," *Journal of Marketing Management* 23 (9–10): 917–28, doi: 10.1362/026725707X250395.

FACIAL EXPRESSIONS

Facial expressions are an extension of your emotions and a key indicator of how you're feeling. It's easy to spot someone who's sad, mad, or happy just by their facial expressions. For example, arched eyebrows tell the audience you're surprised or questioning something. You might use this when revealing a shocking statistic. A frown tells the audience you disapprove or are saddened by something. This may work if you're talking about an idea you want your audience to be moved by.

Smiling is engaging and contagious. If you smile at your audience, they'll probably smile back, which makes you feel more comfortable and likely to continue smiling. If needed, focus on smiling, even if you're unhappy or nervous.

POSTURE

Posture plays an important role in how you're perceived on stage. Correct posture radiates trust, authority, credibility, and confidence. Leaning on the podium tells the audience you're not confident, and this might be interpreted as not being comfortable with the information.

Use these tips to maintain good posture on stage:

- When standing still, keep your feet in one place, shoulder width apart.
- Avoid leaning or rocking from side to side.
- Hold your head high, and keep your gaze out toward the audience.
- Keep your shoulders relaxed, down, and back.
- Keep your hands at your side and never in your pockets.
- Don't lock your knees.

GESTURES

Gesturing too much or gesturing in a way that sends a different message than what you want to communicate is confusing and distracting. Gestures should be appropriate and consistent with the ideas and key points of your speech. You can tell if your gestures are effective by checking what your audience is looking at. If they're looking at your hands, arms, or feet instead of your face, then your gestures may be more of a distraction than an enhancement of your speech.

BODY LANGUAGE BEFORE AND AFTER THE SPEECH

Your presentation begins before you start speaking, and it ends after you stop. Consider that all eyes may be on you as you make your way to the stage to begin your speech. Do you walk up sheepishly? When you exit the stage, do you run or walk off quickly, communicating relief that your speech is over? Your nonverbal movements during this time signal a message to the audience. Make sure it's the correct message.

PART 6

Types of Speeches

"You have to smile, if you expect
anybody to smile back."

—Jonathan Evison

Public speaking comes in many forms, and the success of a speech also varies depending on the expectations of the audience. It all depends on the context. At a wedding, for example, the audience wouldn't expect the best friend of the groom giving a toast to blurt out things that are too personal. Nor would it be appropriate for someone introducing another speaker during a business conference in front of hundreds to criticize that person. What is said and done during a speech to family and friends during a reunion won't be the same as what is said formally in front of many people.

Whatever the occasion, chances are you will be asked to speak, and the speech must fit the occasion. No matter how much time you have to prepare, understanding the objective and methods of any speech will enable you to deliver one the audience will enjoy and remember fondly.

CHAPTER 19

Impactful Welcome and Introduction Speeches

A strong introduction can set
the mood of an event.

The purpose of a welcome and introduction speech is to formally welcome an audience to an event. It marks the start of an occasion, such as a workshop, formal presentation, training session, meeting, film, conference, or celebration.

A welcome speech is important because it can set the mood for the entire event. The goal of the presenter tasked with the welcome speech is to let the audience know that the event has begun and to pique the audience's interest, getting them to eagerly anticipate what is to come.

CHARACTERISTICS OF A WELCOME SPEECH

Welcome speeches in general should be brief—around three to four minutes maximum. If they're any longer, the audience may lose interest. Remember that the purpose of the welcome speech is just an introduction for the activities ahead, which is what the audience came for. Although the audience members will not likely remember the welcome speech, it's an important part of the event, and being selected to give the welcome speech is an important role.

Welcome speeches typically:

- Acknowledge and welcome all the guests, stating the name of the event and host
- Give a brief introduction of the occasion and host
- Introduce the next speaker, if appropriate
- Provide an overview of the agenda or schedule
- Set the mood of the event

To create an exciting welcome speech, include adjectives in your opening language and use specific wording, especially when referring to your audience. For example, rather than just beginning with the typical "Ladies and gentlemen," consider using a more specific way to address your audience, such as colleagues, associates, friends, family, classmates, members, cohorts, or fellow teachers, travelers, or lawyers.

You can use these welcome speech opening phrases:

- "Good morning [or afternoon or evening]. It is with great pleasure that I welcome you to . . ."
- "Welcome, ABC members! Thank you all for . . ."
- "Our desire is to extend a gracious and inclusive welcome to all of you."
- "Let's put aside our differences and instead celebrate what brings us together!"

- "The flags are flying. The balloons are ready for release. It's a great day—one we've been plannng and waiting for."

- "It's gratifying to look around and see so many familiar faces. I know this is a going to be a great conference."

- "Looking around, I can see many familiar faces—past and present peers and colleagues. What a companionable welcome! It's great to see you all here."

- "Many of you have made a huge effort to join us today. On behalf of us all, we are deeply appreciative and offer you our most grateful welcome."

- "Wow, what a gathering we have here tonight! We've got dignitaries, celebrities, fans, and organizational members, all brought together for one cause. Here's an appreciative welcome to you all."

Now, let's look at what a complete welcome speech might include. Remember to keep it short and to the point.

Welcome speech example 1

"Good morning! I'm pleased to take this opportunity to welcome you all to our inaugural open house.

"Today marks the capstone of five years of collective work that we can savor. I'm sure you can all appreciate how far we've come since we broke ground five years ago. Just look around, and I think you'll agree that this building is symbolic of your dedication and passion to make it a world-class healthcare institution.

"We would like to extend our gratitude and thanks to all the role players who have made it possible for this dream to become a reality. Today marks this occasion, the official opening of our new facility.

"I hope you enjoy the rest of the evening's program, and thank you for sharing this special event with us."

Welcome speech example 2

"Esteemed guests, welcome. My name is Cindy Black, president of World Trust United, and it's my privilege and pleasure on behalf of this organization to welcome you here today.

"We are delighted to have you with us to participate and share in our eighth annual Hands of Trust Recognition Day. Thank you for coming. That many of you have traveled long distances to be here serves as a reminder to us all of just how important our work is."

CHARACTERISTICS OF AN INTRODUCTION SPEECH

Introduction speeches are also typically brief, around one to four minutes long. The focus of these speeches should be on the speaker, not on you, the introducer. Your task (as the introducer) is to communicate effectively about the speaker. Your role is to:

- Introduce the guest speaker
- Create a welcoming and motivating environment
- Prepare the audience for what is to come

These speeches are important because they help build excitement about and promote the speaker. With a proper, well-done introduction, the speaker can begin their speech without having to establish their credibility.

Introduction speeches typically include:

- The guest speaker's name and title: Make sure you pronounce the speaker's name correctly. You may need to practice beforehand so you are comfortable saying it.
- The guest speaker's biography: Share a concise summary of significant information that highlights the speaker's credibility and what sets that person apart from the others.

- A surprise: If appropriate, share something revealing about the speaker that further highlights who they are, something the audience may not know about. Examples include awards, challenges the speaker has faced and overcome, and humanitarian work.

Common opening introduction phrases include:

- "Please extend a hearty welcome . . ."
- "I offer a warm welcome . . ."
- "I welcome [use specific name] with all my heart . . ."
- "I'm delighted to offer a happy welcome . . ."
- "Please join me in offering a warmhearted welcome . . ."
- "We're honored with the presence of . . ."
- "It gives me great pleasure to extend to all of you a warm welcome."
- "It's my privilege to address you, on behalf of . . ."
- "On behalf of [name of person, company, or organization], it's my pleasure and privilege to welcome . . ."
- "Here's to a big welcome for our guests, [insert name] and [insert name]."
- "Class [or Colleagues] of '92, please give a warm welcome to . . ."

If possible, talk with the speaker(s) prior to the event to confirm and possibly add to your remarks about them. A phone call or written message before the event also serves to welcome the presenter(s), letting them know that you are looking forward to meeting them and listening to their presentation(s).

Make sure you keep your introduction short and authentic, and avoid reading notes.

CHAPTER 20

Effectively Presenting an Award

Keep in mind the purpose of presenting an award—it's not about you, it's about the winner.

Presenting an award is one of the easiest speeches to give. The focus of the speech is on the person winning the award, not on you, and these types of speeches are typically brief. All you have to do is let the audience know about the accomplishments of the person receiving the award.

Nevertheless, it's still beneficial to plan in advance what you will say and how you will say it. The speech should be appropriate, positive, and cheerful.

Open the speech by commenting on the current occasion and why it's important. For example, the award presentation may be occurring at a company dinner or a yearly conference event that has become central to the organization's history. You could say something about the significance of the award, such as whom it was named after or what it symbolizes. You may also wish to mention the names of past recipients.

Then introduce the award recipient by mentioning what the receiver has contributed to the organization and why they've earned the award. Summarize and praise the recipient's accomplishments. A funny or inspiring quote either by or about the person is a great way to engage the audience and highlight what's special about them. If you know the recipient well, consider sharing a personal story or some insight into their best qualities.

And remember to keep it short, about three minutes or less. The star of the ceremony is the recipient, not you (sorry).

Let's look at a sample speech for presenting an award. In this scenario, you've been asked to present an employee with an Employee of the Year award in front of five hundred people. Here are some suggestions for how you might approach this situation.

START BY CREATING EXCITEMENT

Start your presentation with a strong, positive statement that will grab your audience's attention. You could say, "Each year XYZ Company recognizes an outstanding employee for their superior service by naming him or her as the Employee of the Year. We appreciate everyone's efforts that make this company successful. This person has consistently given 115 percent."

BUILD THE EXCITEMENT

After your strong start, say a few more things about the winner's accomplishments without announcing who it is just yet. This will spark your audience's curiosity. "This year's winner went above and beyond her duties to drive customer satisfaction to new levels we've not seen before. It's because of her strong drive and determination that we have implemented our latest customer loyalty program, resulting in increased sales."

ANNOUNCE THE WINNER

At this point, your audience will be excited to learn who you'll name. "I'm proud to announce that XYZ Company's Employee of the Year is Cyndi Smith!"

CONGRATULATE THE WINNER

You may need to motion to the winner to come up on stage or to the front of the room to receive the award. Depending on the circumstances, at the very least, shake hands with that person, and if appropriate, you might hug them. Then step away from the podium for the person to take the spotlight and say a few words. You might have to step in and respectfully take over, however, if the person rambles on and takes too long with their acceptance speech. A graceful way to do this would be to say, "Thank you, Cyndi. Can we have another round of applause for our Employee of the Year?"

IF APPLICABLE, END THE AWARD CEREMONY

You may need to end the award segment to honor another person or introduce the next speaker. In this situation, you could say, "Thank you, Cyndi, and congratulations, again. Now, let's turn our attention over to John Wellen who will say a few words about . . ."

This example may not neatly apply to all award speeches. Sometimes winners aren't given the opportunity to speak, or you may be presenting awards to several people with little or no time allowed for descriptive introductions. Whatever type of award you're announcing, keep it authentic, emphasizing genuine admiration for the award recipient. Remember, it's about them, not you.

is [your name].

CHAPTER 21

Nailing Impromptu Speeches

How to pull off a great speech with
little (or no) time to prepare

Consider this scenario: You're calmly sitting in a company
meeting listening to your supervisor talk about company
updates. Usually you don't have to say much, as most meetings are led and presented by your boss, with occasional guest speakers. However, about halfway through the meeting, without warning he
gestures to you and grandly announces to everyone in the room, "And
now [insert your name] will talk about the Q3 sales results." All heads
turn your way, and you feel your stomach sinking to your shoes. You're
sure the perplexed look on your face must be obvious to the others.
How should you react?

These kinds of impromptu speeches are common. Adults often find
themselves called upon unexpectedly to stand and deliver during an

interview, at social events, at business and club meetings, and at family gatherings. These surprise speeches can occur in a professional setting, such as being asked to update staff on a software implementation project, or casual settings, such as deciding to give a toast on the spot (yes, you might even volunteer) at your best friend's wedding.

Most of us don't regularly think about giving impromptu speeches. We go about our day without worrying that we'll be called upon to speak on the spot. However, there are many incidents when this can happen. For example, you may be asked to speak because:

- The guest speaker called in sick that day and you're asked to speak in that person's place.
- The scheduled speaker is stuck in traffic and won't arrive until after the event is scheduled to begin. You're asked to fill in until the person arrives.
- You're asked by the speaker to address an audience question.
- You're asked to provide an unexpected update at a department meeting.
- You decide to say a few words, such as an unplanned toast at a family or work event.
- You're asked to speak briefly at a large company gathering.
- You're interviewed by a reporter.
- You're making a live Instagram video.

Unless you have a solid reason why you can't fulfill these types of requests, you'll likely accept them. Turning down a request can make you appear uncooperative or worse (unsympathetic, dismissive, or uncommitted), depending on the situation. The good news, though, is that if you graciously accept, you may be received with praise because your efforts will show that you care, are confident, and are a team player.

Still, accepting the request is just one part of the process. Fulfilling it is another. Let's say you accept the request and then think to yourself, *Now what?* There's no need to fear. You can speak about any topic, despite knowing little about it, and be able to engage your audience. Let's say you're asked to speak about strawberries. You're given no time to prepare and just thirty seconds at the most to present. What do you say? Honestly, it doesn't matter. Just start speaking . . . with confidence, as if you "own" the platform. Maybe you decide to speak on why you like or dislike strawberries. Give your presentation an introduction, body, and conclusion (see Part 2). Here's the formula you will use, even for a short speech:

- **Introduction:** Tell them what you're going to tell them.

- **Body:** Tell them.

- **Conclusion:** Tell them what you told them.

Here's what you might say:

Introduction: "Have you ever bitten into a sweet, vine-ripened strawberry? Strawberries are my favorite fruit, and you should eat them too. Here's why."

Body: "Strawberries are delicious and good for you. The vine-ripened ones, when bitten into, delight the senses. They are also nutritious. They are high in vitamin C and fiber and are low in calories and fat. Strawberries are also colorful and can be used as decorations on other foods, such as on cakes."

Conclusion: "Strawberries are delicious, nutritious, and beautiful, so consider purchasing them the next time you're at the store. You'll be amazed at how they'll enrich your life."

This example is simplistic but applicable. However, you may be tasked with giving an impromptu presentation on a more complicated topic. When faced with this situation, keep in mind that you (fortunately) won't be expected to speak on the topic at hand for very long. Impromptu speeches aren't expected to be involved discussions; in fact, they usually last for only a few minutes. That being said, you can't simply fill those moments with *ums* and *uhs*; instead, you'll need to quickly formulate an outline in your head. Quickly think of what you will say and organize those thoughts into a beginning, middle, and end.

THE INTRODUCTION

Whatever you do, don't start by declaring: "I didn't expect to say anything about that today, but . . . OK . . . I guess I can." Such a comment isn't pertinent and won't make your audience feel that you're a capable speaker. Instead you should approach your impromptu speech as a positive challenge and put a confident smile on your face (even if your insides are turning somersaults).

The best way to begin an impromptu speech is to reiterate the topic about which you were asked to speak (tell them what you are going to tell them). This not only benefits the listeners, helping them to understand the purpose of your speech, it also helps you focus your thoughts on the subject matter.

You could start your speech with a story about a personal experience. (Of course, it should relate to and logically lead into the topic.) It's easier to describe something you know about from experience than it is to talk about something you know little about. Also, telling a story you know well can calm your nerves. (It's easier for the brain to recall and explain than to divulge statistics and facts.)

THE BODY

You can then launch into any details (tell them) related to your topic. You'll likely only need to address one to three points. Providing more than that will be difficult for your audience to remember. It also could cause you to get offtrack (given it's an impromptu speech that you didn't prepare for).

Use structure for the body of your speech. You could share a personal story, a comparison such as good versus bad or before and after, or a timeline focusing on the past, present, and future. You could also choose two main points or features of the topic to discuss in depth.

Validate your speech using facts and supporting statements. Ideally, quote facts from credible sources, especially if they come from recent information. But don't worry if you can't recall any specific facts. You could also talk about related information that you've heard on the news or at a recent conference or meeting you attended. One idea is to ask for a show of hands from the audience. Ask if anyone has experienced something similar or is familiar with the topic. Weaving related, supportive information into your presentation lets your audience know that you're not the only one who thinks this way, which adds credibility to your message.

THE CONCLUSION

In no time at all, you'll find yourself concluding your impromptu speech, after which you can to turn to your host and ask, "Is there anything I missed?"

Still, make sure you finish strong. You may feel compelled to abruptly end your speech simply because you don't know what else to say. However, an audience craves closure because it may otherwise be difficult to tell when the speaker has finished. Make a point to cue the audience that your speech is done. You could end by thanking them for their time and letting them know how they may follow up for additional information. Then pass out business cards or flyers. And again, don't end with an apology or negative remarks about how poorly you felt you presented. Mostly likely the audience didn't pick up on your nervousness or realize you weren't as prepared as you would have been had your presentation been planned.

YOUR EXIT

After you have finished your impromptu presentation, thank your audience for their attention and then give the floor, the microphone, or the podium back to the person who gave it to you or to whoever should get it next. You can look to the host if the occasion has one, or possibly to the event schedule. If there's no obvious recipient, then close the presentation by saying you hope everyone enjoys the remainder of the event.

If you're unable to rid yourself of the spotlight (perhaps your supervisor had to leave the meeting or is unwilling to take back control), you can always open the discussion to questions from the audience. Just be aware that you'll need to respond in an intelligent, honest manner.

If you need to be ready to speak publicly at a moment's notice, keep these tips in mind:

- **Calm yourself.** Close your eyes momentarily and take a deep breath before you begin.

- **If possible, give yourself time to prepare (even just a few minutes can help).**

- **If you don't have time to prepare, then use the time during your walk to the podium to collect your thoughts and plan out your speech.**

- **Silently think about your introduction, or at least the first sentence.**

- **Don't hide behind the lectern.** You'll appear more confident if you directly face the audience, with your feet planted firmly on the floor and arms at your side (not in your pockets).

- **Speak confidently, using a strong voice, as if you have a good command of the topic.**

- **Keep your focus on the topic.** (Remember that your speech should have an introduction, body, and conclusion.)

- **Be brief and to the point.**

- **Don't ramble or say too much or go too far off the subject.**

- **Speak at the audience's level.** Don't use words that are too simplistic or unfamiliar to them.

- **Use positive nonverbals.** As you face the audience, stand tall and make eye contact with them. Smile.

- **Anticipate impromptu speeches.** In situations where you may be asked to present, expect that you will be and plan for it. For example, have a short "just in case" speech prepared when attending a close friend's award ceremony or bachelor or bachelorette party.

- **Learn a few simple impromptu speech templates you can use at a moment's notice.** Here are some:

  - **PREP (Point. Reason. Example. Point):** This one can work for almost any situation. Begin your speech by clearly stating your point and continue by explaining the reasoning for your point. Support it further with an example, and then finish by summarizing your point.

  - **Five "Ws":** Address the five "W" questions: Who, What, When, Where, and Why. This pattern can be easily remembered. (Most of us have had this drilled into our head in primary and secondary school.) This works well for informational and persuasive speeches.

  - **Issue, Pros versus Cons, Conclusions:** This format works well for requests, such as a request for funding, to purchase products and services, or to get approval to move forward with an activity.

  - **Q&A Session:** In some circumstances, you may be asked to fill in for a speaker who, for whatever reason, is not able to present. If you're unprepared for a full formal presentation, you could turn the session into a question-and-answer session (which is essentially a series of small impromptu speeches). This only works if you already have some knowledge of the topic so you can address the questions. The environment must be such that an audience will likely ask them (such as might be the case during a public hearing where those in attendance have strong opinions and are hungry for more information).

- **Don't be hard on yourself.** Impromptu speeches can be challenging, and most likely everyone in the audience is thinking, *I'm glad it's not me*. If it doesn't go well, your audience will probably understand, and if it does go well, you'll impress them even more by your ability to pull off a good impromptu speech.

- **Grab a pen and a piece of paper, whether it's a napkin, envelope, or the back of a piece of paper you have on hand.** If there's time, briefly jot down key and interesting points about your topic. You can use that as a guide when presenting to help keep you on track.

- **Remember that you're in charge of this time.** Being asked to speak on the spot doesn't have to be awful. It can be a fantastic opportunity to take control and make it your own. Being in the spotlight has many benefits, including changing how your audience thinks and feels about something and getting yourself noticed by others (think promotion) who are impressed with your public speaking skills.

- **As you deliver your speech, concentrate on enunciation and tone.** If you're thinking about this, you're not thinking about the eyes watching you. This really works!

And as always, practice! Almost any skill, if not all skills, including impromptu speaking, can improve with practice. The idea is to be prepared to speak well and comfortably at a moment's notice, no matter the subject. You can practice in front of a chair, your pet, a mirror, or your computer. Talk about anything, and don't stop until two minutes are over. If you do this several times a day, within just a few months you'll get more comfortable talking logically and concisely about any topic. I also recommend putting yourself out there and initiating opportunities to speak in front of strangers when the occasion presents itself, such as at club meetings, work events, and even social gatherings. You'll find you get more and more comfortable speaking in front of people.

It's unlikely that an impromptu speech will make or break your career or reputation if you approach it with poise. Don't talk about controversial subject matter, don't use the experience as an opportunity to grandstand, and don't complain or roll your eyes when asked to give your impromptu talk.

Simply pause for a moment and then begin. Before you know it, you'll be patting yourself on the back for a job well (even if hastily) done.

Special Event Speeches

Weddings, birthdays, anniversaries, retirement
parties—make your speech meaningful by
honoring the honoree.

I f you've ever been asked to give a speech for a special occasion, such as a birthday, wedding, anniversary, or retirement celebration, you know that it's an honor and, well . . . also a responsibility. The person hosting the event or the people (such as a bride and groom) whom the event is about will likely request that you speak because you're considered the most qualified, possibly because of your strong relationship with the honorees (for example, a best friend or loved one) or because they expect you to provide a strong positive impact with your speech.

However, being asked also means that you need to consider how to best showcase the honoree(s). Before you get too tense at the thought of doing this, keep in mind that these types of speeches can be the most forgiving as the audience is probably focusing more on the reactions of the recipient(s) than the speaker.

HOW TO APPROACH A
SPECIAL OCCASION SPEECH

When preparing for your next speech for a special occasion, keep in mind theme, tone, and length.

Theme

Your speech will be focused on the addressee(s) of the occasion (birthday, anniversary, or wedding). However, consider the theme most appropriate for the person(s) and event. Here are a few:

- **Accomplishments:** This speech addresses a person's achievements. For instance, "Joe has accomplished more in just ten years than most people do in a lifetime. He's a loving, devoted husband and a dedicated father of three beautiful children, and he summited Mt. Everest successfully. He's also published over five novels with widespread international distribution."

- **Humor:** Your speech can include a touching yet humorous anecdote about the recipient. Here's an example: "When they first met, John lied to Susan about his age, telling her he was five years older than he really was, because he was worried she'd think he was too young. Turns out, she lied to him too, telling him the same. Today we celebrate their thirty-year anniversary. They're both a young fifty years old!"

- **Best wishes:** Your theme could address your best wishes to the recipients. These types of speeches can be applicable to most any type of event, such as a wedding, anniversary, or birthday. Here are a couple of examples: "Bailey, we're all here to celebrate your eighteenth birthday. We wish you all the best on your future endeavors and encourage you to aspire to your dreams." Or, "Tyler and Megan, it's an honor to stand here today in celebration of your marriage. You two are the epitome of a perfect match, and it's been a privilege and joy to see you both grow together in fine harmony. May the years ahead be filled with wonderful adventures and lasting joy."

Tone

The tone of your speech should be reflective of your relationship with the recipients. If you're close to them, your speech could take on a more personal tone, such as telling others about your special relationship with them. However, if you don't know the recipients well or are on more of a formal basis with them, your tone should be supportive and affable, but not intimate. The following are examples of both approaches.

Tone: informal

"I owe my passion and appreciation for the outdoors to my mother. She taught me how to respect nature, including how to live off the land with just the clothes on my back. Her years of unwavering dedication and devotion to educating others on how to survive in the wilderness and wilderness preservation have made a lasting positive impact on many."

Tone: formal

"Tony Milton will be remembered for his tireless commitment to inspiring and facilitating learning for his students and the community. On this thirty-fifth anniversary of his employment as an educator at this institution, we honor and thank him for being a pivotal part in helping so many achieve their dreams."

Length

Typically these types of speeches are short, usually between one to three minutes. The purpose is to provide a brief acknowledgment of the recipient, applicable to the purpose of the event and your relationship to them.

However, these speeches may last longer if they mark a very special occasion, such as a fiftieth wedding anniversary or a retirement party. In this case, a longer speech may be necessary to adequately honor the person or persons, sharing any background about them that is applicable to the celebration.

SPECIAL OCCASION SPEECHES: THINGS TO KEEP IN MIND

When giving a speech at a special event, you may need to first get the attention of the audience who may be noisily chatting, laughing, dancing, or eating. A common and usually efficient method for this type of event is to use a microphone so everyone can hear you. Clicking a champagne glass with a fork or knife can sound nice, but this passive action won't likely be heard or noticed unless the room is already dead silent. In this situation, you could say something like, "Good evening, everyone! May I have your attention for a few minutes? Please join me in a toast . . ."

Your toast should be as brief and concise as possible, especially if you've interrupted the party to request that they focus their attention on you. They'll probably appreciate your toast but are also eager to get back to what they were doing (dancing, eating, laughing, and so on). You only need to say a few heartfelt sentences.

No matter how well you know the recipient, keep your speech clean and upbeat. Avoid using the speech as a time to disclose secrets or share inappropriate stories about something you've shared or experienced with the recipient that shouldn't be shared with others. Unless the event is a roast among close friends and family, all information shared should be positive to keep the tone and mood upbeat and respectful. Your recipients want to feel good and not embarrassed during the event. You might say something like this: "I'm very fortunate and grateful to have known Carrie through these years. She's one of the most caring and selfless people I know. She's been a dear friend of mine since we first met in high school. As roommates in college, we somehow survived on McDonald's chocolate chip cookies and Chicken McNuggets."

SPECIAL OCCASION SPEECH TEMPLATES

While your speech should be original and expressed with heart, here are some templates to get you started. These follow the same introduction, body, conclusion formula discussed in detail in Part 2.

Wedding speeches

Wedding speeches are usually given at the reception after the wedding in honor of the newlyweds. They are usually short and often quite sentimental.

- Express how thrilled you are to be at the wedding, and thank the bride and groom (and their parents, if appropriate) for inviting everyone to be a part of their special day.

- Share a personal memory appropriate for the occasion that will be emotionally significant to the audience.

- Offer encouraging (possibly moving) words of advice for the couple's future together.

- Finish with the official toast, raising your glass and saying, "A toast [Cheers, Hats off] to Ron and Janet!"

Wedding speech examples

- In your introduction, express your affection toward the couple: "I love you both so much!"

- In the body of your toast, express a lovely anecdote about the couple's relationship and how awesome they are (as a couple). You can also talk about the context of their relationship. This should be the bulk of your speech. For example: "May you always be happy, joyous, and in love," or "This proves how madly in love you two are. You're an inspiration to us all," or "To the couple we all know, admire, and love with all our hearts." You get the idea.

- To conclude, make the toast. "Everyone drinks!", or "A toast to the two of you on this special day," or "We toast to your health and happiness."

Birthday speeches

Toasts are sometimes given during a birthday celebration. These speeches are typically short and sentimental, inspirational, or humorous.

If you know the person well, think of something special about that person you can share. For example, you might begin by saying, "Sharon, we have put in many miles on runs together, and you are always one step ahead. You continually challenge me. Here's to many more runs where you whip my butt! Let's raise our glasses! Cheers to a great birthday for this strong lady!" Another option when toasting someone you know (as reported on hallmark.com) is to share something semi-personal, such as a hobby, and turn it into a compliment. For example: "Happy Birthday, Jason! We wish you all the best. We love you even more than you love skiing!"

If you don't know the person well, a warm compliment always works. Try to personalize it as much as possible. For example: "Cheers for a wonderful birthday to a great man who has achieved so much. Tonight, surrounded by loved ones, colleagues, and dear friends, we all wish you the best for many years to come."

Start the speech by stating something warm and positive about the person. Follow that with supporting comments, such as describing how that person is special or what you wish for that person. End the speech with a final greeting. Following is an example of a birthday speech.

Birthday speech example

- **Introduction:** "Here's a toast to the noblest [bravest, strongest, wisest, most caring (fill in the appropriate wording)] person I know."

- **Body:** "On this special day, may you be reminded of how much you mean to all of us. You have helped so many with such devotion and conviction, spreading happiness across the globe. We love you dearly for all that you are."

- **Conclusion:** "Wishing you all the best with many smiles for years to come. Happy Birthday! Cheers!"

Anniversary speeches

When offering an anniversary speech, consider congratulating the couple and then commenting on significant events in their lives. Strive to keep the mood light and focus on a few highlights of their lives together.

Start the speech by saying something attention-getting. You could begin with a question or a quote—or if you know the person well and feel it's appropriate, tell a joke or share something funny about them. The body of the speech should follow naturally from the introduction. If you started with a question, then answer it. For example, you might begin your speech with "What is love?" You could follow that by saying, "According to the *Oxford Dictionary*, love is defined as . . ." End your speech with a compliment or message of goodwill. You could also end with a quote or even a thank you. Below is an example of a wedding anniversary speech.

Anniversary speech example

- **Introduction:** something attention-getting such as a question or quote. "What is love?" or "True love never dies."

- **Body:** "If you ever need an answer to the question what is love or what is the key to a successful marriage, then look no further than John and Susan." (Continue with a story about them, perhaps an example of their devotion and love for each other.)

- **Conclusion:** a positive, goodwill statement. "Happy anniversary, dear friends!" "Thank you, Mom and Dad, for being a great example of love," or "I would like to thank you . . . for putting up with my. . . . You are my number one fan, my love, and my rock. I love you!"

Retirement speeches

Retirements are about endings and beginnings, and whatever you say about a retiree should be heartfelt and descriptive of the retiree's contributions in the workplace.

Your retirement speech should be short. Keep in mind that the audience, whether coworkers, close friends, or family, are there to celebrate and honor the retiree. Your job is to express gratitude, care, and appreciation, as appropriate. It's important that your speech emphasize the effect of the person's contribution to the workplace and their profession.

Retirement speeches can take place during an impromtu assembly of coworkers who meet at the local pub on a Friday afternoon, a more formal sit-down dinner at a posh restaurant, or a company-wide meeting held in a large auditorium. The following template can help you consider a retirement speech appropriate for any situation.

Retirement speech example

- **Introduction:** Begin by welcoming everyone and making a few short introductory remarks about the retiree. For example: "Thanks, everyone, for coming today. I'd like to start by saying a heartfelt good-bye to someone who [share something important about that person—a short description of their contribution to the company or their role or term of service]."

- **Body:** Follow with key points about that person's career. You could tell a story about something special and important they did or summarize highlights of their service over time and how things have (positively) changed as a result of their work. The depth of this section depends on the type of job and seniority of the role the person held. However, don't make your speech too long; concentrate on a few main points. For example, "Jim joined our company thirty-five years ago, fresh out of college. He started in the stockroom when our company consisted of less than twenty employees and we were barely making ends meet. He quickly revolutionized our approach to stock control. His contributions continued throughout his tenure. One of his biggest contributions was [summarize]."

- **Conclusion:** Finish your speech by expressing gratitude, goodwill, and positive remarks about that person's future. You could end by proposing a toast, if appropriate. For example: "We are going to miss you, Alice, but we take comfort in knowing that if you put as much devotion into your retirement as you did during your tenure with this company, you will no doubt have many great and rewarding years ahead. A huge thank-you for all you've done and for being an incredible colleague and friend. We wish you all the best in the next chapter of your life. Here's a toast to a long and happy retirement!"

These types of special events can be emotional and meaningful. A robotic-sounding speech without any emotion reflected in your voice and words will not be well received. You'll find that the words will fall into place when you're authentic and speaking from your heart.

Finally, do a self "fit" test before you speak up in front of a crowd. Are you clear headed? Too many alcoholic drinks may calm your nerves or make you feel inclined to speak up, but you may not come across as successfully as you intend. That pre-check may prevent you from saying the wrong words or slurring your words in front of a captive audience.

Raise your glass for the official toast, if applicable; it's a common practice. Also it's good manners to take a sip afterward as a symbol of the toast.

CHAPTER 23

Acing Employment Interview Presentations

Delivering a speech authentically, clearly, and
confidently for an interview can position you as a
strong candidate

At some point in your career, you may be asked to give a presentation as part of your interview for a job. I've had to do it more than once. Granted, I was applying for positions where speaking in front of an audience (such as for an instructor or training role) was the primary part of the job, so this type of interview made sense. However, employers also use this as a test to see how well a candidate can address others in a public speaking situation and how well they perform under pressure.

If you're already adept at public speaking, these types of speeches may not feel so challenging to you. Whatever your experience and confidence level with interviewing and officially speaking in public is, do keep in mind that interview speeches are distinct from others. As with any speech, though, it can go well if you know what to expect and plan accordingly.

If asked to present at an interview, find out these facts in advance:

- Topic
- Length (minimum and maximum)
- Attendees/audience (and find out who they are and why they will be there)
- Expectations
- Evaluation of you
- Method of presenting (i.e., online or in person)
- Location, including the room size and setup
- Access to presentation materials, such as a lectern, computer, overhead projector, microphone, and so on.

PLANNING

Most likely you'll be asked to present so your potential employer can see your skills and demeanor. They don't necessarily care about the topic you're speaking about. They may ask you to speak about broad topics such as giving instructions, key challenges you've experienced in past roles, your teaching or leadership style, or your goals for the new post.

If this scares you, don't panic! Do your homework and practice. Here are some suggested ways you can prepare. To start:

- **Discover as much as you can about the company.** Talk to someone who works or has worked at the company to learn about the environment, including any challenges and opportunities facing the company, the position you're applying for, and anything else important to know.

- **Use the internet to research what you can about the company.**

- **Find out the specifics of what the employer is looking for in a candidate.** Address how well your qualifications match the requirements listed in the job description.

Then plan out and develop your speech. Follow this guide:

- **Identify the key points of your speech.** Keep them to around three (typically you won't be given more than thirty minutes to present).

- **Know what kind of visual aids you'll use and practice using them.** Consider distributing a one-page handout (given after your speech unless it's used as part of your speech, such as a worksheet to get your audience engaged and enhance their learning—more on that later).

- **Make sure your presentation targets the audience.** Don't make it too simple or too technical. Either way can make you appear as if you're patronizing them.

- **Practice your speech enough so you're confident in presenting it within the allocated time.** Since there may not be a clock in the room, or one that you can easily see, bring something with you so you can see the time.

- **If you will be presenting by a video conference, practice with someone you know beforehand.**

- **Relax and be authentic and professional.** Your speech shouldn't feel awkward to you or your audience (those interviewing and evaluating you).

PROVIDING A HANDOUT

Consider providing a one-page handout, given before, during, or after your presentation, primarily so your interviewers will remember you and your speech. A handout can be a way for you to stand out from other applicants. However, handouts can backfire if not done well. Here's a guide for effective handouts:

- **Use a professional format and design.** Your handout shouldn't appear as an unorganized and poorly designed document that will reflect negatively on you and your qualifications.

- **It should showcase the highlights of your presentation.**

- **It should be clear and correct.**

- **Strategize when to distribute it.** Make it available before you begin if it's necessary for your audience to have in preparation of your speech. Distribute it during your speech if it's a part of your speech. Give it out at the end so your audience isn't distracted by it during your presentation if it serves as a reminder for your key points.

EXPECT THE UNEXPECTED

It could happen. You walk in to give your speech and find that the laptop with internet access you were promised doesn't work or the internet is down or any number of other technical difficulties. This can be frustrating, but if you plan for the unexpected, then you'll more likely be prepared with a backup plan. Your interviewers will also appreciate how well you demonstrate your ability to address unexpected challenges.

At the end of your presentation, clearly conclude by summarizing your key points before inviting questions from the interview panel.

CHAPTER 24

Delivering Powerful Pitches with Confidence

Believe in your message and say it
confidently to more easily meet and make
connections with people.

A short thirty-second (or less) speech, also referred to as an
elevator pitch or elevator speech, is the most common type
of presentation. Most adults are asked, "What do you do?" at
any function, especially in networking environments and when meeting people for the first time. In casual situations, there's less pressure
to answer the question well. However, in professional settings, the
response can make an impact on one's credibility.

Many people don't like networking because they aren't comfortable
speaking; they don't know what to say. However, by spending some
time preparing your pitch, you'll find it much easier to meet people
and have more meaningful connections.

WHAT IS AN ELEVATOR PITCH?

Elevator pitches are succinct and persuasive, typically completed within about thirty seconds—the time it takes to ride an elevator up or down. These pitches are meant to communicate a message quickly and effectively.

Elevator pitches are often used at the beginning of a conversation, meeting, or presentation. It's therefore important that they're presented well to engage the audience up front and make a positive impression.

Think of an elevator pitch as similar to a television commercial. Your pitch should be catchy enough to capture the audience's attention, and it should be relevant so they're not tempted to change the channel or hit the mute button on their remote.

WHEN TO USE AN ELEVATOR PITCH

Elevator pitches are used to communicate a proposition or idea to others who may have a stake in its success. These speeches are typically used to pitch a product or service and generate interest in you or your company. They're also used to meet others, initiate conversation, spark interest in potential clients or customers, sell and generate interest in a new idea to your boss and other decision makers, and tell others what you do for a living. They're also used for job applications at career fairs when you introduce yourself to a potential employer; at an interview in answer to the statement, "Tell me about yourself"; or when cold-calling employers for a future position.

Done well, polished elevator pitches can impress and engage an audience. These short speeches, however, can be challenging without adequate preparation. The chance to elicit interest can quickly diminish if your proposal isn't communicated clearly and quickly. Busy professionals are often bombarded with ideas and proposals daily and don't have the time to wait for lengthy details. Many great ideas are lost opportunities because of poor presentation.

Whether you're attending a job fair, career expo, mixer, or other type of networking event, having a well-prepared pitch is a great way to make yourself stand out from competitors and other potential employees.

TYPES OF ELEVATOR PITCHES

Think about an occasion when you may have to give an elevator speech, and tailor your remarks for each potential situation. These are great to have rehearsed and ready. Below are a few types.

Professional networking pitch

Professional networking events are often perfect opportunities to make your pitch to a listener, especially when seeking possible investors, clients, or business partners.

Career fair pitch

A career fair is a recruiting event where employers meet with job seekers to provide information about general career opportunities as well as specific details on current openings. Career fairs are a good way to meet and connect with representatives from a variety of companies and organizations while also improving one's networking and professional skills.

Most people attend a career fair hoping to stand out from the crowd. These are competitive events. Why should the listener take the time to hear your pitch? It's therefore important to open your pitch with a clear introduction, explaining who you are (your unique skills) and what you're looking for.

Getting a new client pitch

Elevator speeches are also used to acquire new clients for you and your company. While the basic points of an elevator speech still apply, it should reflect the service or product you offer. Start by identifying what you and your company do and how the listener can benefit.

Job interview pitch

If you're seeking a new job position, keep in mind that the employer is spending a lot of time talking with different candidates. Recruiters and employers often assess the viability of a candidate within the first few minutes of the interview. Many will start the interview with "Tell me [us] about yourself." This is usually aimed at relaxing you into the interview and getting an overview of who you are. Your reply shouldn't be lengthy and unrelated. You won't impress the interviewers with a lengthy description about your obsession with Star Trek (unless they share the same passion or the job you're applying for relates to the same industry). While the content of your speech should be unique to you and your personal background, several basic guidelines should be followed:

1. The pitch should not be longer than thirty seconds.

2. The pitch should clearly define the skills and benefits you would bring to an employer.

3. The pitch should address your clear goal, and it should tie in with the company you're applying at. You could also ask the employer about his or her goals and how you can help meet them as an employee.

Most of your pitch should highlight the top experiences and skills of your academic and work history, finishing with an explanation of why you want to work for the company and your career goals that could be achieved through the position.

Personal pitch

If you're promoting yourself, such as seeking funding for a new project, consider approaching potential investors by integrating your strengths into a personal elevator pitch. Let the listener know how your past accomplishments prove that you're a worthy investment. Explain who you are, what you offer in a professional context, and what you intend to achieve in the future.

Venture capitalist pitch

Venture capitalists are most often from professional private or public firms looking to invest in various types of businesses and start-ups to make a high rate of return on their investments. When crafting an elevator pitch for potential investors, focus on your business prospects and long-term goals. Since an elevator pitch should be under thirty seconds long, the speech should be treated as a short introduction showing why your business would be a worthy investment.

The pitch should clearly describe your business idea in a concise manner. Venture capitalists spend a lot of time listening to business pitches from a wide array of individuals, so make sure your business idea stands out from the rest.

CREATE A SUCCESSFUL ELEVATOR PITCH

If you've attended a business networking event, you've probably been bombarded by elevator pitches. Few will stand out in your mind, and fewer still will result in sought-after contacts. What sets these pitches apart, and how can you ensure that yours will generate interest and conversation?

A strong elevator pitch immediately grabs the listener's attention and quickly, clearly, and concisely communicates the message, leaving a lasting, positive impression on the receiver. Successful pitches typically address a solution to a problem and the benefits targeting the receiver. For these to be effective, you need to provide just enough relevant and compelling information that's of interest to others without overwhelming them with too much.

Steps for creating a successful elevator pitch

To create a successful pitch, follow the steps listed next. You may need to vary your approach based on the environment and audience to sound authentic and target your message accordingly. Update it periodically as needed.

Step 1: Identify your goal and objective.

Start by identifying your goal. For example, do you want to generate buzz about a controversial topic or generate leads for your products or services? Perhaps you want to gain support for an idea or just want to feel confident explaining what you do for a living.

Step 2: Identify the problem and issue.

Write out the key problem and need. Keep your audience in mind as you do this. For example, if your goal is to land a job interview, then consider why the company should hire you.

Step 3: Define a solution.

Next write out your approach to solving the problem. Consider how the approach differs from others and how easy it is to adopt. Show the benefits of your solution, including saving time and costs and improving quality and revenue. Tell what problems you solve and offer a vivid example, such as, "Through support services and training, we help about ten thousand people every year find employment."

Step 4: Describe how the solution will be implemented.

Write out how, what, and when the work would be implemented, including who will do the work. Give a concrete example or tell a short story showing your uniqueness, with emotional appeal and strong impact. For example: "Since we began our program five years ago, we've helped thousands of individuals, including families with small children, find gainful employment and locate shelters, getting them off the street."

Step 5: Describe your unique selling point.

Identify the unique selling point or proposition that identifies what makes you, your organization, idea, product, or service unique. Consider the special services or solutions you offer and the advantages of working with you and your organization. You might say, "What makes Leap and Service different is that we have a successful advocacy program called DEEMSOL that helps many homeless individuals to access shelters and healthcare."

Step 6: Describe yourself.

Explain who you are and your role, and include your location: For example, "I'm John Smith, executive director for Leap and Service, a global nonprofit providing career counseling to the homeless."

Step 7: Identify the call to action.

The pitch is not an end in itself; it's designed to initiate interest. The call to action should therefore provide clear next steps on how people can act on your message. Consider the most wanted response after your elevator speech. Do you want a business card or a request for your business card, a request for more information, or a referral? For example: "Can I contact you to set up a meeting?"

Step 8: Put it all together.

After you've written out each section of your speech, put it all together. Then cut out anything that isn't important. Add content and revise as needed to easily adapt to the audience and situation.

Below is the structure of a typical elevator pitch.

COMPONENT	ADAPTED TO PITCH
Attention/Opening Statement	Hook (a statement or question that piques the listener's interest to want to hear more)
Introduction	What you (clearly) have to offer
Body	Benefits; what's in it for the listener
Conclusion	Example that sums it up
Residual Message	Call to action; ask for something of your listener

Here's an example of a complete elevator pitch:

> "I noticed that you're looking for a candidate with strong
> experience in [fill in area of expertise]. My name is Jim, and
> I'm excited about the new position with your company. At my
> last position, I raised our success rates right away by focusing
> on _____. I maximized profits quickly and efficiently,
> identifying what was slowing down the business operations. I
> can do the same for you in this new position. Here's my resume.
> Would you be willing to meet with me next week for an official
> interview?"

Step 9: Practice

Practice your pitch, reading it aloud several times until you're comfortable saying it without referring to notes. Also, time yourself and revise as necessary to keep it twenty to thirty seconds. If possible, practice in front of people, or at the very least in front of a mirror, or use a camera to record yourself.

Step 10: Create different versions of your pitch.

Go back and revise your pitch according to different possible scenarios where you might use it. That way you'll be able to easily target your speech for different audiences.

Elevator pitch guidelines

As you go through each step, also consider the following guidelines when building your pitch.

Start with a question

Relevant questions can be an effective opener for immediately getting someone's attention. Ask thought-provoking questions that can be answered with a yes or no (possibly by a show of hands or asking them to think about it silently) to get your listeners involved without losing control of your pitch.

Keep it authentic

The overall pitch should come across as being natural to you. It shouldn't feel like it's a persuasive pitch, which can be an instant turn-off to people. Try to convey your message in a way that's spontaneous and sincere.

Support your statements

People can quickly see through the smoke if your message isn't compelling. Make sure your statements are backed with solid proof, such as testimonials, examples, or references to third-party reviews and awards.

Be clear about what you want

Identify what *you* are interested in, whether it's employment or building an existing business. Knowing this will make it easier for you to craft your pitch and portray it and yourself in a way that makes sense. For example, if you want to pursue employment as an artist, emphasize your related skills and experience rather than talk about the time you worked in an unrelated industry or profession.

Make your argument compelling

Your proposition or messaging should clearly emphasize audience benefits and be credible. Focus your message on how your solution provides the best value for your audience. Be specific, although brief, about the benefits and support or resources needed for success.

Be excited about your pitch

Your audience won't be excited about your pitch if you aren't. Smile when you present it, and even better, be passionate about it. Enthusiasm is infectious.

Be clear and concise

Use language that is to the point. Don't ramble on with unnecessary wording. And remember to stay away from fancy words thinking they will impress your listener. You should also skip any acronyms that may be unfamiliar to your audience.

Keep it conversational

Your speech should come across as natural and not as an obvious "pitch," which can turn off your audience. Consider using a soft-sell approach to show you're sincere. People aren't usually ready to buy and commit to something immediately. Instead, they may want to know more about how a problem can be solved or how you can help them with their situation.

Make the message about your audience

Make sure your message clearly targets the audience. They won't be interested in your speech unless it's clear to them how they'll benefit from it.

Be confident

Putting yourself out there to a stranger can make you feel vulnerable. However, appearing confident will make a difference in how your listener perceives you. If you sound like you're confident in what you do and want, your listener will more likely believe it too.

Use body language strategically

Pay attention to how you approach and interact with others. Your body language greatly affects your message. Do your best to appear approachable and inviting. Look the listener in the eye, face them, keep your hands unfolded and out of your pockets, and smile.

Have business cards and other takeaways available.

You never know when the right opportunity will present itself to deliver a successful pitch. If done well, you may end up swapping business cards with someone who can help you down the line.

ELEVATOR PITCH TEMPLATES AND EXAMPLES

Below are templates and examples of various types of elevator speeches.

Elevator pitch for networking

- **Start by identifying yourself.** This sentence lays the foundation by telling people who you are.

- **Next describe your specialty.** Identify the problem or issue and how you provide the solution.

- **Then describe how you are different.** State what makes you better and why you're unique. Establish credibility, build value, and provide proof (such as testimonials or third-party facts).

- **Finish with a call to action.** Tell your audience what and how to act.

Example elevator pitch for networking

- **Introduction:** "Good morning [afternoon, evening]. My name is . . . I am a . . . specializing in . . . for [name of company or organization].

- **Body:** "I help/provide [describe what you do]. I [or my company] has [describe what you or your company has done to help others (solved problems, saved money)." You could throw in testimonials and statistics to support your credibility, such as, "We have been in business for thirty years, maintaining a triple A+ rating by the Better Business Bureau."

- **Closing:** End with a call to action, such as, "Can I get your contact information and follow up with you about . . .?"

Elevator pitch to an investor or customer

Consider these questions to prepare your elevator pitch for an investor or customer:

- What's your topic, product, or service?
- Who are you?
- Who's your target market?
- What's your revenue model (if applicable)?
- Who's your competition (if applicable)?
- What are your advantages (you, company, or other)?

Then, apply an appropriate structure. Here's an example:

- Introduce yourself with a friendly demeanor and start with an attention-getting question or statement.
- Once you have your audience's attention, focus on who you are and what your company does.
- Explain what you can offer by demonstrating how you, the company, or your products have solved problems in the past. Offer examples and explain how your points can benefit the listener.
- Describe the unique benefits of your products/services/other and explain any advantages your company may have over the competition.
- Close your pitch with a call for action.

Example elevator pitches to investors and customers

- Highlight what makes your company unique: "Our approach is unique. We conduct an extensive skills analysis with every client to develop a training system specific to their needs. As a result, on average, 95 percent of our clients are satisfied with their training."

- Capture attention with a question: "How does your company handle the training of new hires?"

Elevator pitch to an investor

"Cocolucious will be Aspenville's first 100 percent organic coconut freeze stand. We'll sell coconut milk freezes in a variety of fruit mixtures including coconut banana and coconut mango. The coconut milk–based product market is among the fastest growing in our state since it offers a health-conscious alternative to milk-based products. During this past year, we've opened five stands with exponential sales growth. Would you be interested in being part of an enterprise with projected $1 million in sales over the next five years? I can send you my business plan by email."

Elevator pitch to a potential customer

"Good morning [afternoon]. Would you like a free sample of our organic gooseberry protein bars? With each sale, we donate 40 percent of our profit to the Child in Need program. Each bar is packed with nutrients and contains no preservatives or artificial coloring or flavoring. Here's a coupon for your first purchase."

"Nice to meet you, [name]. My name is John, and after ten years of working at dental offices, I've taken the plunge to open my own office. If you know of anyone looking for a new dentist, please send them my way. Here's my card."

"My name is Tina, and I run a landscaping company. We've been in business for over twenty years with a long list of strong customer testimonials. Not only do we guarantee your satisfaction, but our staff—not an automated system—personally answers the phones."

Example answers to "What do you do?"

> "I help companies increase their revenue by writing email newsletters that entice people to buy something again and not unsubscribe."

> "I make web and WordPress sites and create graphic designs for small jewelry companies, helping them increase sales by at least 25 percent in one year."

> "I create illustrations for fashion-related websites and brands. My passion is coming up with creative ways to express a message and drawing illustrations that people share on social media."

Elevator pitch for a job interview

Here are two possible structures of an employment pitch:

Employment pitch structure #1:

- Introduce yourself.
- State your goal, relevant to the position and organization.
- State a strength or skill related to the position or organization.
- Follow that with a supportive accomplishment proving you have that skill.
- Describe your employment objectives—what you're looking for in the job.
- Describe how you can immediately benefit the company.

Employment pitch structure #2:

- Start with an attention-getting statement.
- Follow this with the benefits you would bring as a possible employee or partner.

- Move on to emphasize what makes you stand out (describe your strengths).
- Briefly state your related experience, background, and skills.
- Explain how your qualifications benefit the listener. Focus on what you're looking for or your career goals and how your experience makes you stand out from others.

Example employment pitches

"When I noticed your company was going to be here [Career Fair], I knew I wanted to stop by as [company] is a place I've wanted to work. I saw on your website that you're hiring for [role]. I believe I would be a great fit because . . ."

"Can you use an experienced database administrator with solid experience helping companies . . .?"

"My name is _____. I'm a student at _____. majoring in _____."

"I want to [career goal]. I'm [strength], which I demonstrated when I [accomplishment]."

"I'm looking for a job where I [job details]"

"I can immediately benefit your company because [how]"

"Ms. Smith, I'm graduating cum laude this spring with a degree in set design. My work was recently showcased, winning first place at the Elena Consortium. I'm interested in learning more about and expanding my skills in the movie industry. Would you be willing to consider me for a position as an assistant this summer? I can send you my resume and references."

"I recently graduated from college with a degree in communications. I worked on the college newspaper as a reporter and eventually as the editor of the arts section. I'm looking for a job that will put my skills as a journalist to work."

"I have over ten years of experience as a tax accountant, working primarily with small and midsize firms. If your company is ever in need of assistance with its taxes, I'd be thrilled to offer consulting."

"I'm a financial services advisor for DBNW based out of New York. I'm looking to relocate closer to my roots and join a small firm. I specialize in family financial planning."

CHAPTER 25

Presenting Online

Viewed by a select few at a business
webinar, or shared with the world, make
sure your online message is clear and your
presence is as intended.

L ive streaming and video conferencing have become mainstream. According to their latest figures, YouTube has over one billion users.[11] Facebook draws a large presence as well. Facebook's full year 2018 financial report says that there are over 1.52 billion daily active users.[12] Social Report reports that, as of January 2018, over 100 million hours of video are watched on Facebook Daily.[13] Anyone can

---

11   https://www.youtube.com/yt/about/press/.
12   "Facebook Reports Fourth Quarter and Full Year 2018 Results," Facebook Press Release, January 30, 2019, https://investor.fb.com/investor-news/press-release-details/2019/Facebook-Reports-Fourth-Quarter-and-Full-Year-2018-Results/default.aspx.
13   "The Latest Facebook Statistics," Social Report, January 25, 2018, https://www.socialreport.com/insights/article/360000094166-The-Latest-Facebook-Statistics-2018.

share their voice, and many have become famous through this platform. This medium has created a new genre of celebrity. Companies also use video, including live streaming, to grow their presence and ultimately their business. Easy and widespread access to video conferencing means that anyone can sell anything and forge a relationship with any customer.

There are no real rules for video conferencing and presenting in any form over the internet. Practically anything goes and will work, depending on the scenario, setting, audience, and any number of other variables. For instance, Joe Shmo's novice YouTube video of his pet dog doing amazing tricks may draw millions of viewers. Even if the video quality is poor, viewers are captivated by the dog. However, not everyone has a pet with such unique talents. More often, presenting this way successfully requires some strategy and planning, especially for professional use.

Consider these examples:

- **Early one Wednesday morning, Molly is reviewing her notes and presentation materials before her scheduled video conference with her colleagues.** She plans to review the slides and presentation content with her peers for some final feedback before she presents them later in the day in an online webinar to over fifty potential customers.

- **Jon heads up a big project that involves employees located in the United States and across the globe.** Although he'd prefer to meet with them in person, he sets up an online presentation so everyone can participate and collaborate during the same meeting.

- **Jake, a reporter for a third-party tech business publishing company, is attending an international conference with over three hundred vendors and 100,000 attendees.** His boss asked him to record a series of ten-second videos showing him briefing the latest technologies being showcased at the exhibition. The videos will be included in feature articles and posted on the company's website. In order to effectively record, he must contend with a lot of people, noise, and various distractions.

- **Chelsey is excited and anxious for her upcoming screening interview held by video conference for an international company with headquarters located in Geneva, Switzerland.** Chelsey lives in Los Angeles, California. She's very interested in representing the company as the director of sales for the Western region, USA. Her meeting is scheduled for 6:00 a.m. Pacific time, which is nine hours behind Switzerland, where her interviewers are located. If she does well during the live, online interview, the company will fly her to Switzerland for further interviews.

(i) TIP

Regardless of which online method you use, make sure it's done well. Unlike an undocumented department meeting of just a few people, anything posted online can be permanent and viewed by many. Make sure your online presence is exactly how you want it.

These examples show the convenience of video conferencing. Have you had similar experiences? Connecting with an online audience may involve different circumstances, considerations, and skills to pull off effectively. With online presentations, you may not get to see or hear your audience. It can be an adjustment to speak to a device, especially when you don't know who's on the other end watching and listening to you. It may seem as if you're alone at your office or in a room by yourself speaking to a device, but real people can hear and see you, including all your nonverbal movements.

Consider the following guidelines for delivering an effective online presentation.

SELECT THE BEST MEANS OF PRESENTING

A successful online presentation can produce many benefits. Organizations often use them to advertise their company or network and build credentials and exposure. There are many ways to host live online events, so it's important to consider various factors, including the costs, options, benefits, features, accessibility, compatibility, function, and how well you can achieve your goal for the event. Two common formats for presenting online are broadcasting live events and webinars.

You will want to pick the right one for your topic and audience. Here is a brief overview of these two options.

Broadcasting or live video streaming

Companies have found live video streaming to be a powerful tool to spontaneously share and promote their business and connect with their audience, allowing access to live events and creating feeds that can be beamed worldwide, ultimately boosting business. Live video also satiates the public's growing sense of a now-or-never kind of urgency, an ever-increasing hunger for immediate information. However, it comes with limitations, including the necessity to immediately capture an audience and deal with the imperfections in video quality. There's a big difference in the impact of a poorly done versus a professional-quality video presentation. People may move in and out of shots, the camera may shake, and the narrator or presenter may be hard to hear. But capturing a live streaming video is also easy—you just record. The recording can be uploaded immediately to a social media site, website, or blog.

Webinars or web conferencing

Webinars or web conferencing are interactive, real-time, online platforms for virtual meetings, web conferences, and lectures, allowing interactivity among attendees. Multiple media can be applied simultaneously, including live video streaming, slide presentations, and chat. Webinars can be done in real time and recorded for later viewing.

PLAN YOUR PRESENTATION

For professional live videos, do some planning. Live broadcasts should have a purpose. Know what your broadcast is about and what you want to say. Prepare a list of talking points to refer to if needed.

USE THE RIGHT SOFTWARE

Your online presentation will only be as good as the quality of the software you use. Webinar and live video streaming programs such as Facebook Live, GoToMeeting, or Zoom work on almost any system and allow users to upload content (such as slides), view each other in real time, talk and chat in writing, and record meetings for later viewing.

Know how to use the software

Don't wait until the scheduled online meeting or presentation to log on to the software program. It's embarrassing and frustrating, especially if you're running the session, when you can't log on or are uncertain of how to use the program or how to upload and show your slides after you've already logged on. Instead, allow yourself plenty of time before you deliver your presentation to get familiar with the program. Play around with all the tools available until you're comfortable using them. If possible, log on and practice using a second monitor, or practice with someone you know so you can test it out on both ends.

CHECK YOUR ENVIRONMENT

Are you using the webcam in your office or at home? Check that the environment captured on camera represents the image you're going for. The camera of whatever device you use captures everything in its lens, which includes whatever is hanging or shown on the wall behind you, the chair you're sitting on, or the items on your desk or in a nearby bookcase. The camera may also pick up any background noise, which can distract from your meeting or presentation, especially if you're streaming a live event where a lot is going on in the background. Unless the background noise and activities are an essential part of your video, consider these factors to establish a professional setting on camera:

Limit distracting background noise

Set up the environment so there's no noise (or minimal noise). Close all windows and doors and silence any electronics (such as your cell phone).

Use a professional background

If you're presenting at the office, do a test of what the camera captures. The camera shouldn't pick up anything distracting, misleading, offensive, or sensitive (such as patient information) or anything that might affect the audience's impression of you (such as a messy desk). If you're filming at home, make sure kids and pets don't accidentally walk into the room or can be heard in the background. Remove any family photos, dirty clothes, or anything else that can be a distraction or too personal in nature.

CHECK YOUR APPEARANCE

Dress and groom yourself appropriately from head to toe for the occasion. You may think the audience will only be able to see your head, or see you from the waist up. But consider that, for whatever reason, you might have to unexpectedly stand or switch positions, and the audience will be able to see your lower half. (Don't wear your pajama bottoms or anything you wouldn't want your audience to see.)

Wear a solid-color shirt, preferably light blue. Solid colors usually show better on camera than multicolored prints, as certain patterns create optical illusions on camera. Also, wear colors that contrast with the background. For example, a dark color shirt or dress works well if your background is a light color. Avoid wearing the same color as your background (i.e., a black shirt with a black background). White clothing isn't the best choice as it reflects light.

USE GOOD LIGHTING

You should be well illuminated without distracting shadows. Create a lighting balance, ideally being illuminated from the top, sides, in front of, and behind you. Professional lighting setups can work well, but you don't necessarily have to spend a lot of money to create effective lighting. Any standard lamps and even sunlight can create the desired effect. Place a light or two pointed down at about a forty-five-degree angle in front of you. This could be a desk lamp or a clamp light. You can also use overhead lights for top-down lighting. Again, the lighting should be positioned so you, the subject, are illuminated. Use subtle lighting from behind you. If it's too bright, you may appear washed out and shadowed.

Filming yourself outside presents many challenges. It may be difficult to control and manage the environment—background noise (airplanes, cars, neighbors), the lighting, and so on. You may appear too dark if the sun is behind you, or you may have to squint if the bright sun is in your face.

Finally, avoid filming in front of an open window with the sunlight streaming in behind you, as you'll appear shadowed.

USE THE BEST POSITIONING

Avoid sitting or standing too close or too far from the camera. If you're too far away, the audience may not be able to see you and may have trouble hearing you. Conversely, if you're too close to the camera (within one foot), just your head will be within the frame, which might be uncomfortable to your audience (and they'll see every little detail of your face). The best position is usually about three feet from and centered in front of the lens, so you're seen from the shoulders up.

MAKE EYE CONTACT AT EYE LEVEL

Place your web camera at eye level. The camera is the eyes of your audience. If you look down at the camera, it will appear to the audience as if they're looking up at you. Conversely, if the camera is higher than eye level, you'll appear to your audience as if you're looking up at them.

You'll appear more confident if you're at eye level. You may need to adjust the height of your seat or place your computer on something (such as a stack of books) that raises it up enough for you to be eye level with the camera.

Unless you are being recorded so it appears as if you aren't being recorded (i.e., such as when interviewing or being interviewed by others), maintain eye contact with the camera. Avoid looking down or to the side to read your notes or script. It will appear to your audience as if you're no longer focusing on them when you look away.

Keep this in mind during any live stream as well, especially if you're holding a recording device (i.e., a cell phone) that can be difficult to keep steady.

MAKE IT EASY TO ATTEND

Don't make it challenging for your audience to join the meeting. Set up your meeting using a platform that doesn't require participants to sign up for an account or download anything. Provide clear, easy-to-understand instructions for accessing the site and your presentation.

RECORD IT

Consider recording your presentation, including any audience questions and responses. You may want to use these recordings to help build your business and your portfolio.

OPEN WITH A CAPTIVATING INTRODUCTION

Viewers will form a first impression quickly, so it's important to grab their attention with a captivating introduction. Refer to Chapter 11, Opening Strategies, for ideas on how to begin your speech. Only apply those that will work in an online or video format. For example, compelling statistics, testimonials, stories, quotes, and thought-provoking questions work well.

INCORPORATE VISUALS

Use visuals such as slides to leverage your presentation to better engage your audience. Research shows that people use just 3 percent of their brain for hearing and 30 percent for processing visual information. Viewers are more likely to stay engaged when visuals are shown during an online presentation.

BEGIN AND END ON TIME

Live meetings sometimes start a few minutes late to make certain everyone has arrived. However, this is not recommended with online meetings and presentations because people may be at their desk at work and will quickly move on to other pressing tasks. They may not have the patience or the time to wait for your session to begin.

SET THE CONTEXT

Start the web presentation with a welcome slide that lets attendees know what to expect. Review the ground rules; go over how to use any special features such as chat and instant polls. Make the audience comfortable with the process, and they'll be a lot more likely to participate.

AVOID CONFUSION FOR LATE JOINERS

People may not join the live session right away. Start strong, with a clear introduction, but avoid cramming everything important within the first few minutes. If you are interviewing or conversing with others, every so often, say their first name and rephrase the topic and question as applicable to let viewers know what's going on. For live events, if it's a small group, briefly acknowledge and introduce the newcomer.

KEEP IT REAL—BE LIKABLE

Consider the video as a means to really connect with your audience. Don't try to market yourself or sell a product. Instead, relax, smile, and be yourself. If you are broadcasting live, your video will be unedited and raw, which viewers may perceive as more authentic. Avoid sounding robotic, trotting out bullet points without any expression. If you can't see them, pretend the camera is a real person and talk more conversationally and authentically. You'll appear more inviting and engaging. Keep in mind that you are on camera, so don't pick your nose, blow out your cheeks, or close your eyes except to blink.

BE CLEAR AND EFFICIENT

With online presentations, it's important that your voice sounds clear and vibrant. In live presentations, the audience uses your body language, eye contact, and facial expressions to gain a better understanding of the content. However, with online presentations, especially if the audience can only hear you, they'll rely solely on your voice. Make sure you speak loud enough and articulate well, with a good tone and pace. Smile throughout, as this also affects the quality of your voice. You want to sound enthusiastic.

BE CULTURALLY SENSITIVE

When talking to a global audience, keep cultural references in mind. Use of colloquial terms and jargon should be minimized.

SCHEDULE A TIME FOR QUESTIONS

If your online presentation is live, schedule and set aside time for questions. Let your audience know at the beginning of your speech when they can ask questions. Include the question section in the agenda so your audience knows what to expect.

BUILD RAPPORT WITH YOUR AUDIENCE

Focus your presentation on your audience. It should be clear to them how they benefit from what you are sharing. Keep your presentation engaging and stimulating. Imbed humor and attention-grabbing graphics and illustrations as appropriate. If your presentation is structured for audience involvement, motivate and encourage them to participate with questions, polls, and messaging.

USE A HEADSET MICROPHONE

Most built-in microphones on a laptop are low quality and produce poor audio that sounds muffled and distorted and causes your voice to sound tinny and muted. Instead invest in a headset microphone you plug into the computer.

RESPOND TO AUDIENCE COMMENTS

If you allow audience comments throughout your speech (which can increase engagement), consider addressing the comments as they feed in. You may need assistance from someone off camera to filter the comments and direct the most important ones your way.

CLOSE STRONG

Like live, on-site presentations, virtual ones also need a strong closing to motivate your audience to act on or believe in something. Make it easy for the audience by giving them solid, clear next steps, such as providing an online link to a signup form or online store.

Use the worksheet that follows to prepare your next video and live streaming presentation.

Video and Online Presentation
Planner Worksheet

CRITERIA	NOTES
What are your webinar or video objectives and desired outcomes?	
What hosting platform will you use?	
Who is your audience and why would they be interested?	
What is the title of your presentation?	
What is your audience call to action? What do you want them to do with the information?	
What audio requirements are needed?	
Will you need visuals? If yes, assess the type and function. How will you effectively manage them during your speech?	
Have you done a trial run prior to the event, giving yourself adequate time to improve and revise your presentation as needed?	
What will you wear, and where will you present or record?	
Are there any distractions in the background that will be captured on camera?	
Is your video capture set up correctly so you and your visuals are easily seen by your audience?	
Do you know how to use the software?	
Do you have a backup plan in case the software doesn't work for live sessions?	

CHAPTER 26

Presenting to Large Groups

Methods vary on presenting effectively to an audience of five, twenty, one hundred, or millions of people, but one thing remains the same— getting your message across.

P resenting to a large audience, which in this context refers to an event involving more than one hundred people in attendance, such as at a conference or seminar ("millions" of people refers to public presentations of online viewers), necessitates different strategies and considerations. Unlike small venues, such as small department meetings that may last just an hour or two, large events can last all day, involving a formal program consisting of several speakers.

Presenting to a large audience can be challenging for even experienced speakers because there are several things they must be concerned about:

- Being compared to the speakers before and after them or any other speaker in the lineup

- Losing control of an audience

- Effectively adapting their speech to a diverse group of people

- Not being able to sufficiently gauge how well the audience understood and valued the presentation

- Doing something embarrassing or feeling inadequate in front of many people

Despite these concerns, presenting to a large audience can be quite rewarding. Consider the following benefits:

- Builds credibility: Speaking at a large event is an excellent way to improve your credibility.

- Expands your network: You'll have a wider opportunity to network. You may find that people will seek you out during breaks and after the presentation to talk to you.

- Builds your brand: You'll increase your exposure.

- Increases sales: In one setting you can reach a large audience to promote your products and services.

- Changes the world: Well, at least in chunks. Presenting to a large group can be an effective platform for spreading revolutionary ideas.

Here are suggested factors to consider when presenting to large groups. Keeping these things in mind will help your presentation be a success.

POSITIONING

Where will you position yourself in front of the audience? A large event will often have a lectern available for presenters. It may be placed off to the side or somewhere toward the center of the room. Find out in advance if you'll have control over where it's placed and if not, how you'll work around it.

DISTANCE

You'll be in a large room that holds a lot of people, and it may be difficult to see those in the back (and vice versa), especially if the seating isn't tiered. The back-of-the-room folks will have to rely on what they hear, unless there are cameras that project you on screens placed where those in the back can more easily hear and see you.

EQUIPMENT

You'll almost always have professional sound and audio-visual equipment at a large event. You may be asked to provide your presentation in advance or have your visuals loaded and ready to use when you get to the stage. You might also be provided with a wire microphone (or not, so make sure you check and plan accordingly).

VOICE

Use more variation in your tone of voice than you would normally. Just as when you're speaking on the phone and people have fewer visual cues, use your voice in a presentation to emphasize your thoughts and feelings.

EYE CONTACT

In a large room, you may not be able to see the audience, especially if the lights are dimmed with the spotlight only on you. However, they can see you, so make sure you still scan the room, smile, and look at your audience. If you're projected on the large screen, your face and eye contact may be even more visible. It will appear to your audience that you're engaging with them personally.

PRESENCE

A common issue when presenting to large groups is the vast distance between the presenter and the audience, causing a feeling of disconnect between them. The presenter can feel isolated on stage, and the audience may feel as if the presenter is unattainable.

Here are some strategies to better connect with the audience when they feel far away.

- **Make your presence known.** Don't hide on the stage or be incognito when the audience is filtering in and taking their seats. Walk up and down the aisles and greet people. Smile and make eye contact with people as they enter.

- **Display the topic of your speech and your name on an overhead visual or on a flyer placed on everyone's seat.**

- **Manage where people sit.** Encourage people to sit up front as they filter in.

- **Introduce yourself at the beginning.** Don't assume everyone knows or remembers your name and who you are.

QUESTIONS

Large venues aren't generally conducive to audience questions. People take on the "small fish in a big pond" belief and prefer to keep quiet rather than speak up in front of a large crowd. To provoke questions, let the audience know when they can ask them, and then encourage them to do so at that time. You can also use a slide to show your contact information at the end of your presentation so people can reach out to you with questions after the event is finished.

AUDIBILITY

It's imperative that the entire audience can hear you well, especially if not everyone can adequately see you (such as those seated on the far sides and toward the back of the room). Make sure the volume on the microphone is at the right setting. Avoid shouting, which can come across as aggressive and difficult for an audience to listen to. Most microphones for large venues are set to amplify a speaker's voice spoken at a normal volume.

Working with a large audience presents a different set of challenges than presenting to a small audience. However, proper planning and management of the process results in a powerful presentation with a positive outcome.

CHAPTER 27

Presenting to Small Groups

You may be more approachable when
presenting to a few people. Be prepared
to engage with the audience.

Presenting to an audience of up to ten people is vastly different than presenting to large audiences. Small presentations are much more common in business activities that may include training seminars and workshops, reports to management, pitches to new clients, and project updates with colleagues and clients. When presenting to a small group, the goal typically is to get people to take a specific action, such as approving a request or proposal or implementing a specific program or process.

When presenting to a large audience, the speaker often is standing behind a podium or on an elevated stage with access to a projector, microphone, and other presentation-related tools. However, presenting to a small audience often involves the speaker standing just a few feet away from the participants, who generally are seated at a conference table, and often there are limited presentation tools available. Presenting to a small group of people can be successful with thoughtful planning.

Consider the following tips when presenting to smaller groups.

KNOW YOUR AUDIENCE

Small groups often possess a tighter focus than large ones, and your content may need to do more than just motivate. Be relevant and passionate about your topic and understand specifically how it applies to the group and its concerns. Prepare in advance by finding out how much the audience members know in advance; understand what they want and need from you.

UNDERSTAND SMALL GROUP DYNAMICS

Unlike large audiences, small groups often interact closely, depending on each other to solve a problem, make a decision, or achieve a common goal (as in executive meetings, workshop environments, and sales meetings). You shouldn't talk nonstop. Instead, you should pause, ask for questions, and give the audience a chance to comment; consider conducting an activity to get them talking to one another. Presenting to smaller groups should be more like a discussion where you, as the speaker, are in charge.

PREPARE FOR AND ENCOURAGE MORE DIRECT INTERACTION

Expect a smaller group to be more willing to engage, since you're more accessible. If you have enough time and it's appropriate, have the group members introduce themselves and share their expertise. You can call upon them later to share their experiences with your topic.

WATCH THE NONVERBAL MOVEMENTS FOR CUES

You can often easily tell how well people are keeping up with you by watching their facial expressions, especially in a small group setting. If you see puzzled looks as you go through your handouts, for example, adjust your presentation speed to their comprehension speed. Slow down if you see people fidgeting and not paying attention to you or looking confused. Ask for understanding at those points and review.

PLAN IF AND WHERE TO STAND

Plan whether you'll stand or sit—or a combination of both—during your presentation. Standing when others are seated puts you in a power position. This can work well when you want to come across as credible and authoritative and when you're presenting information without requesting input. However, it may feel uncomfortable or inappropriate depending on the circumstances. Sitting is effective when you want to provoke equal participation, such as when holding a brainstorming session or creating an environment where no one is inferior or superior. You could do both—stand when you need to explain or illustrate something on the whiteboard, for example, and then sit back down for the group discussion.

KNOW WHERE TO SIT

If your session is held where everyone is seated, you'll need to select the best, most effective place to sit. Seating shouldn't be random; it can play a big role in the success of your event. Here are some guidelines that have been shown to make a difference.

Sit at the corner next to a decision maker

Studies have shown that you'll more likely to get agreement by those in authority if you sit next to or adjacent to them at the corner of a table. Conversely, those seated across from each other are typically in a more adversarial position.

Sit where you can maximize eye contact

Sit where you can best see everyone, such as at the head of a table. If you sit in the middle at the side, it may be difficult to see those on either side of you. You'd have to crank your head from left to right, and even then, you may not be able to see everyone, as someone may be seated slightly forward or backward and blocking the view of others.

Sit where you can maximize your vocal power

Room acoustics and seating arrangements affect how well your voice is heard, so sit where people can best hear you and you're facing and can make eye contact with everyone (such as at the front of the table). How you sit impacts your body's ability to speak powerfully; poor posture restricts the diaphragm. To maximize your voice when sitting, firmly place your feet shoulder width apart, evenly weighted on the floor, and sit upright with your back straight and your head held up high.

Lean forward and back

Experts suggest leaning in slightly when you speak to appear as if you're engaged with your audience, and then leaning back to appear more approachable, which can help when you want your audience to ask questions and submit input. Be careful, though, not to appear too relaxed—this can make you appear less authoritative.

Presenting from a seated position versus standing and choosing the most strategic place to sit at the table depend on your relationship with the audience and your goal for the session. Ultimately, success comes down to how well you can engage with the audience.

PART 7

Strategies for a Great Speech

"The success of your presentation will be judged
not by the knowledge you send, but by what the
listener receives."

—Lilly Walters

You have a solid script of your speech that you feel confident about, and you have rehearsed it to the point you feel you can present it well. You've also addressed the necessary preparations for the venue, including having adequate seating, lighting, and refreshments, and you are familiar with the layout of the room and location where you will present. Is it enough? What happens if nerves set in and you panic just before you begin your speech? What happens if your audience doesn't react as you'd hoped, or you are faced with someone who disrupts the flow and dynamics of your event?

These are some things to consider before giving your presentation. It's very helpful to think though all possible "what ifs" so you know how to effectively manage them. For example, if you anticipate allowing time for audience questions, consider the type of questions asked and how you will address any for which you don't have answers.

If you are faced with an angry and disruptive person, or someone who seems to try and dominate your speech, know in advance how you will handle this person professionally and ultimately positively.

It's important to remain positive throughout your speech so you don't let anything that comes up unexpectedly disrupt your thinking and dampen your emotions. You'll want to avoid slipping into a cycle of negative thought, especially just before you begin your speech.

Self-sabotaging thoughts lower your confidence and can harm your ability to achieve what you are capable of doing.

Remember, your speech isn't over after you have "stepped off of the stage." Consider also what happens afterward. For example, you may want to follow up with the participants, so you'll need to know how to reach them. If you want to know the effectiveness of your speech, you'll need a way to measure your success.

CHAPTER 28

Overcoming Fear

Fear isn't bad. It can motivate you to do well,
and it can be managed and prevented using a
few simple techniques.

H ave you ever felt weak in the knees and sick to your stomach when speaking in front of a live audience? If you answered yes, then you're not alone. In his article "The Thing We Fear More Than Death," author Glenn Croston states, "Surveys about our fears commonly show fear of public speaking at the top of the list."[14] Even comedian Jerry Seinfeld joked that if you go to a funeral, "you're better off in the casket than doing the eulogy." Public speaking may not be the most common fear. However, most people don't rank it high on their list of desired activities.

---

14 Glenn Croston, "The Thing We Fear More Than Death," *Psychology Today*, November
29, 2012, https://www.psychologytoday.com/us/blog/the-real-story-risk/201211/
the-thing-we-fear-more-death.

For many years, the thought of putting myself out there and being the focal point of so much attention as a presenter sickened me. Despite pep talks to myself just prior to presenting, I would still feel that rush of nerves well up; I would become flushed and dizzy, and I would experience brain fog. Those feelings seemed to fuel more anxiety, and it affected my voice.

Have you ever attended a meeting or workshop where the facilitator asked the audience to "go around the room" and take turns standing up and sharing something about themselves? This exercise should be easy, with little thought required. However, I found this activity unpleasant, and I would spend the time leading up to my turn thinking about what I would say rather than listening to others. By the time my turn came, I had already become a ball of nerves and could barely squeak out a few faint words. I was sure every person in that room was thinking about how terrible I was doing. Does that sound familiar?

The idea of being embarrassed can send many of us into lockup mode when addressing an audience. We lose our breath, our thoughts seize, and we become expressionless. We may also feel light-headed and break out in a sweat, forgetting parts of or even our entire speech. It can be a terrifying experience; however, these experiences can be prevented.

Several years ago, one of my students came to my office to tell me that he wouldn't be able to speak in front of the class (a required assignment) and asked if I would instead take partial credit for a script of what he would have said, with accompanying slides. He told me he was too afraid to speak in pubic and couldn't stand the thought of being embarrassed. Fortunately, he brought this up early in the semester. I encouraged him to take an active role in all the class activities leading up to the presentation that was due later in the semester, because by that time, he might feel more confident about presenting. Over the course of the semester, students worked in groups, often giving mini presentations to each other, so they could practice presenting and build confidence speaking in public. At the end of the semester, this student didn't back down and gave a well-organized and professional, although not flawless, speech.

You can overcome your fear of public speaking by understanding how and why you fear it.

WHY PEOPLE ARE AFRAID OF PUBLIC SPEAKING

Theories vary about why people are afraid of public speaking. A report published in the *Journal of Communication Education* found that the fear of public speaking often stems from how one thinks, feels, and acts based on their emotions.[15] A similar study, as reported in the *Journal of Communication Research*, found a significant difference in body sensations between varying levels of anxiety-sensitive speakers.[16] Contributing factors include the following.

Physiology

Our autonomic nervous system is hardwired to fire in response to a threatening stimulus. You most likely have heard of the phrase *fight-or-flight*, which refers to our built-in safety mechanism of self-protection. When a threat is activated, chemicals such as adrenaline, noradrenaline, and cortisol are released into the bloodstream, affecting the way we think and our reactions. Studies have shown that people sometimes respond, seemingly instinctively, to danger with a show of strength they didn't know they had, such as running faster and lifting heavy objects, or performing acts of bravery, such as running into a burning

---

15   Bodie Graham, "A Racing Heart, Rattling Knees, and Ruminative Thoughts: Defining, Explaining, and Treating Public Speaking Anxiety," *Communication Education* 59, no. 1 (2012): 70–105, https://eric.ed.gov/?id=EJ875338.

16   Penny Addison, Jaime Ayala, Mark Hunter, Ralph R. Behnke, and Chris R. Sawyer, "Body Sensations of Higher and Lower Anxiety Sensitive Speakers Anticipating a Public Presentation," *Communication Research Reports* 21, no. 3 (2004): 284–290, https://www.tandfonline.com/doi/abs/10.1080/08824090409359990.

building to save an animal or a person. However, the fight-or-flight response to fear can also trigger a racing heartbeat, an upset stomach, muscle tension, and an inability to concentrate. The same can apply to a fear of public speaking and interfere with our ability to speak comfortably in front of an audience.

Doubts

People often fear public speaking because they have a negative view of themselves as a speaker. They label themselves as not being good at public speaking and worry about how poorly they may perform, as if their audience is evaluating them as a presenter. Common concerns include:

- Forgetting what to say
- Speaking too quickly or quietly
- Sounding or looking stupid
- Boring the audience
- Tarnishing credibility
- Having an idea or proposal rejected

Doubt is fueled by varying situations affecting confidence, such as inexperience with public speaking, status differences (speaking to an audience of higher status), and speaking to an audience you are unfamiliar with.

To overcome any fear of public speaking, start by identifying specifically what you're afraid of. Then, assess the reasons for your fears and brainstorm what might be done to overcome those fears. Consider these solutions.

Forgetting what to say

This can be prevented by knowing your topic well, especially a topic you feel passionate about. Learn as much as you can and assess what inspires you most about the topic. Then practice, not just by memorizing your speech but by practicing what you know in a conversational form, as if you were speaking to your best friend. If you're still worried about forgetting key information, write down a few key words of your speech in outline format on a notecard that you can easily refer to and use it as a prompt for quick reference if needed.

Speaking too quickly or quietly

Having your voice waver and seize up in front of an audience can be scary, frustrating, and embarrassing. To prevent this from happening, stand up straight and face your audience. Correct posture can help you better control and project your voice. If you still feel that you won't be able to speak clearly, stop speaking momentarily, take a drink of water (have a glass close by), take a deep breath, smile, and begin again. Most likely, your audience will have no idea that you felt nervous.

Sounding stupid or looking stupid

I grouped these two fears together because they're mostly in your head; they are sentiments not shared by your audience. Keep in mind that your audience wants to benefit from your speech. They don't want their time wasted and will be focused on how the message might positively impact them. They're there for a purpose and won't know as much as you know about your topic. If you're passionate about your material, know it well, and speak and address your audience with confidence, you'll appear credible and knowledgeable— and not at all stupid!

Boring the audience

A great speech doesn't require the speaker to be a skilled comedian or entertainer. Effective presentations effectively target the audience. Your presentation can be engaging and dynamic by:

- **Emphasizing audience benefits:** Clearly address how your audience will benefit from the message.

- **Demonstrating your passion and enthusiasm:** A smile can be infectious, and so can laughter. Showing enthusiasm and expressing passion and excitement will engage your audience who will want to feel the same positive vibes.

- **Being genuine:** Don't assume you need to be someone you're not. You'll feel more comfortable and will more easily connect with the audience if you're just yourself.

Tarnishing credibility

A natural concern of public speaking is the effect it has on one's credibility. Putting yourself in a vulnerable position publicly comes with risk. You might think, *There's no risk to my credibility if no one knows I'm not good at public speaking.* However, keep in mind that public speaking can be an effective means of building credibility. Start by creating a rapport with your audience by respecting them and aligning your speech to their needs. Use solid evidence and embody (believe in) your message to strengthen it.

Rejection of an idea or proposal

The fear of failure is especially common to those who are risk-averse. People often judge their abilities and fear rejection when asking people to invest their time, money, and energy in something with an uncertain outcome. However, you can improve your chance of approval by demonstrating that your idea or request is concrete and reasonable and relates to your audience's goals and aspirations.

Keep this in mind: Your nerves are not visible to the audience. You may feel afraid and stressed, but those feelings are internal. In most cases, your audience has no idea about the turmoil going on inside in your head and gut, so keep pressing on with your speech and don't tell them how you feel. They may empathize with you if you do confess, but it can also make them feel uncomfortable and change the energy of the room. They may have been focused on the content and not on you, so if you let them know you're nervous, they may then direct their focus on you and your performance. If you do show obvious signs of nervousness, such as a shaky voice, keep pressing on without talking about your nerves. Again, the audience may or may not notice. If they do, most people appreciate the challenges of your role and will understand and be sympathetic. They're there to learn from you, and they genuinely want you to succeed.

It's natural to feel nervous when speaking in front of a crowd. We've all been there. Celebrities, teachers, politicians, and seasoned presenters in general feel nervous before an important speech. However, nervousness is not a weakness. It means you care and want to do well. It's energy that can be channeled productively, and it can motivate you to deliver a strong speech.

STRATEGIES TO MANAGE AND PREVENT NERVES

A savvy business leader who often speaks in front of an audience once told me how he combats nerves. He holds his breath for as long as possible before he gets on stage. He said that the act of holding his breath causes him to "shut down" internally and makes his uneasiness disappear. While I don't recommend that you practice this (I don't want anyone to pass out from holding their breath too long), there are other methods that might work just as well. Use one of these nerve-busting strategies as needed.

Take deep breaths

Adrenaline and anxiety cause one to take shallow breaths, which can result in light-headedness. If you find yourself in this state, take a few deep breaths to get more oxygen to the brain and (hopefully) calm yourself down.

Smile

Studies have shown that smiling triggers a chemical reaction in your body that is a natural relaxant. Even just fake smiling can almost instantly change your mood. Have you ever seen studies or been involved in an experiment where a group intentionally laughs and keeps laughing? At first, their laughter is forced, but then almost everyone participating ends up laughing for real.

Drink water

It's important to keep hydrated so you don't end up with a dry mouth, which can make it difficult to articulate well. Even the act of picking up a glass and taking a sip can work as a diversion to how you're feeling, causing you to calm down.

Give yourself a massage

Do a brief self-massage on your hands or head or shoulders; this technique has been shown to calm nerves.

Give yourself a pep talk

Give yourself a pep talk, using uplifting, positive words. If you tell yourself you'll do well, you'll start to believe it. You'll also feel more confident, and your positive wording will become a reality.

Visualize the best scenario

Visualize an audience of people who are receptive and enthusiastic about your speech. See them smiling, and see yourself delivering a dynamic, strong presentation. Cement this visual in your head.

Pause

Just before you're ready to speak, take a moment to collect your thoughts, smile, take a deep breath, and look at your audience. This last moment will feel peaceful, and the action also helps calm and prepare the audience, who are eagerly anticipating your speech.

Slow down

If you find yourself sprinting out of the gate, talking way too quickly, focus on slowing down. The slower pace will calm you.

Move around

Move around during your presentation to dispel some energy and relax your nerves. If you nervously stand in one spot, you might lock your knees, which can cause you to faint, so get moving.

Get active

If you feel anxious before you speak, get some exercise to burn off built-up cortisol. Cortisol is secreted by the adrenaline glands when you are anxious or nervous. High levels of cortisol heighten emotions and limit creativity and the ability to process complex information, making it difficult to read the audience. Take a walk, hit the gym, go for a run, or do any intense short workout that gets your blood pumping before your speaking engagement. You may find that immediately following your workout your mind seems sharper and you can articulate well—that is, unless you worked out so hard that you're out of breath.

Focus on your audience

Most presentation nerves are the result of the speaker worrying about doing poorly. Instead, focus your attention on the audience. Remember, the speech is about them, not you. You'll find that your nerves go away when you remind yourself that the audience is there because they want to benefit from what you tell them, and you're just the medium for how that information is shared.

Get calm, do relaxation exercises

Relaxation techniques involve controlling your breathing, lowering your heart rate, and reducing tension in your muscles. If possible, a few minutes before you go on stage, do some exercises to help you relax. Here are a few ideas:

- **Tightly clench every muscle simultaneously (or you could just focus on the muscles in specific parts of your body, such as your hands or feet) and hold for a few seconds, then release.** You can do this while sitting in a chair and it won't be noticeable to others (that is, unless you make a weird expression while doing so).

- **Stand with your feet planted firmly on the floor shoulder width apart.** Raise your hands high above your head and then lower them to your sides. Slowly bend over from your hips and let your arms flop down in front of you, like a rag doll. Swing at your hips back and forth a few times, still folded over. Shake your head back and forth as well, and then slowly rise, one vertebra at a time, back to a standing position. Do this a few times.

- **Meditate for five minutes before you present.** Close your eyes and focus on your breathing and nothing else. This is best done in a quiet place with little distraction.

Change your beliefs about fear

Challenge your beliefs about your fear of public speaking. Assess why you're fearful, and consider reframing your negative thoughts, which are untrue and not supported by facts, into positive, proactive statements. For example, instead of telling yourself that "you're boring and can't speak well," focus on how your audience will benefit from what you share with them. Imagine your audience actively listening to what you say, not focusing on how well you're presenting.

CHAPTER 29

Using Gimmicks and Props Effectively

Engage your audience using objects to
support your topic and aid in understanding
your message.

Pulling a bunny out of a hat at the start of a presentation may immediately get the audience's attention, but does it really help you achieve your goal? Gimmicks and props can be useful during a presentation because they are great ways to engage your audience, but they must be used at the right time and place and in the correct way. Props and gimmicks can make concepts concrete. They can be used to distill an idea into a memorable image. You may not remember much of the textbook used in your high school chemistry class, but you probably remember the experience of physically combining chemicals in a lab. Physical representations of concepts and ideas help people understand and remember.

However, not all props are effective, and some may appear *too* gimmicky. Props should align with the message appropriate to the audience. Done correctly, they can engage and interest your audience and add clarity to your message.

GIMMICKS

Presentation gimmicks, defined as "a trick or device intended to attract attention, publicity, or business," can be effectively used in presentations, but they are not without risk, especially if you've never tried them before and don't know your audience.

Gimmicks, done well, can be very effective at grabbing attention. They can make a presentation fun and engaging and be one of the highlights the audience will remember. However, if they fail, they can fail big, and audiences will also remember that.

Gimmicks, in general, can also be defined as "a marketing strategy designed to attract customers." Gimmicks such as offering free products, coupons, or steep discounts are commonly used in sales and advertising. In retail, stores often advertise an item at a low price (i.e., ten pencils for ten cents each) to get customers into the store (hoping they'll buy the sale item as well as other regularly priced items). Whether used for presentations or as marketing tactics, gimmicks draw people in and can capture an audience's attention.

If you're considering using gimmicks in your presentation, consider these ideas for positive results:

- **Change of pace:** Break up the action with picture-only slides or multimedia (i.e., an audio or video clip).

- **Use a natural voice:** Speak authentically as you present your gimmick. Your audience is smart and will quickly question your credibility if you come across as being too pushy or not genuine. Speak to your audience as you would like to be spoken to.

- **Keep it relative:** Avoid using gimmicks that contradict your message. Enticing a potential customer with a free sample of a donut when all you sell is sugar-free products would be confusing to your audience.

- **Explain audience benefits:** Be clear how your audience will benefit. For example, if you offer coupons or samples of a product, highlight how these are valuable for the audience.

- **"One more thing":** Surprise your audience with something they weren't expecting, such as a bonus or benefit related to your message.

- **Give out a souvenir:** Hand out a souvenir or something to take away that relates to your message. This could be a pen, a mug, a key chain, or something with your logo, contact information, or a message you want them to remember.

PUBLIC SPEAKING PROPS

Props are like gimmicks in that they're used to capture the audience's attention. However, they're external items used as part of the speech. Props provide the proof of your words. The old saying "Seeing is believing" rings true here. Your message becomes more believable when the audience can see something that reinforces your words.

When to use props

Use props that support your topic and aid understanding of your message. Props should add value to what you want to demonstrate.

I once attended a presentation given just before lunch. The presenter was promoting his specialty food business, and he focused most of the presentation on the quality and success of his food products. He showed several pictures of people eating and enjoying the food, as well as emphasizing the healthy ingredients. At the end of the speech, the presenter passed out one of the company's energy bars with a coupon that could be used to order it online. Most of the audience wasted no time ripping open the packaging and eating the bar. The strategy worked, not only in fulfilling an audience need but also because it was directly applicable to the message.

How to use props

Props can be used in a variety of ways, often only limited by practical considerations such as weight, size, and technology requirements (i.e., access to an outlet). Here's a checklist to work through when considering your prop options:

- **Contingencies:** If you use props, make sure you plan for possible contingencies. For example, if you give out free samples, plan how many you'll need so you have enough for everyone. Also consider how you will give them out.

- **Integrate:** Seamlessly integrate the prop into your speech, showing and telling as you go.

- **Amount:** Don't overdo it by using too many props. Keep it simple, and bring only what's needed to persuade your audience and drive home your key message.

- **Backup plan:** Have a backup plan for any mishaps, such as failed batteries or a broken part.

- **Describe:** Clearly describe the prop as you show it and make sure the audience understands how it relates to your message.

- **Use:** Make sure you know how to use the prop. It can be difficult to convince an audience of the benefit of a device if you can't figure out how to use it during your speech.

- **Test:** Check your prop prior to the event to make sure it works.

CHAPTER 30

Addressing Audience Questions

Anticipate audience questions so
you'll know how to manage and
address them effectively.

One of my clients dreaded the question-and-answer session
of a presentation and would do anything he could to prevent
being asked questions. He told me he would stay awake at
night anticipating audience questions, and this caused him to fear the
whole presentation. To avoid the questions, he'd complete his speech
quickly, with little pause from beginning to end, hastily leaving the
stage when finished. "I don't provide my audience any opportunity to
ask questions," he told me.

People fear audience questions because they're afraid they'll be
embarrassed if they don't know the answers. They're afraid they'll
lose control.

You don't have to dread dealing with questions. Managed well, they can be advantageous to your speech. Here's how.

First, the audience doesn't want to trip you up. Most questions are genuine. Your audience sincerely wants to know more. If you get a lot of questions, you should pat yourself on the back—this means your audience listened to your speech and was engaged enough that they wanted to know more.

Second, use questions as an opportunity to further sell and inform your audience. The questions give insight into what interests the audience, and this is information you can use strategically to glean more data that can help with your business.

MANAGING CHALLENGING QUESTIONS

You may be asked challenging questions or periodically have the rare audience member who seems to have an ulterior motive. Managing questions well can be one of the most challenging aspects of presenting if you're not in control of the process. "Expect the unexpected" from the audience.

For example, you may have an audience member who is a know-it-all, is pessimistic, has a million questions, loves the spotlight, or wants to prove you wrong. Not knowing how to effectively manage these situations can be frustrating, discouraging, and embarrassing, especially if you feel that it negatively affects your credibility and the overall outcome of the presentation.

However, these situations can benefit you.

"I love the opportunity to be challenged by the audience when presenting," says Tom Iselin, a nonprofit strategist, speaker, and principal of First Things First, a nonprofit consulting company. "Their questioning shows interest. If one person dominates with many questions and information, I'll use it as a launching point to elicit others' feedback and questions. For example, I might say, 'Great point, John. Does anyone have something to add to that?' 'Cathy, what is your experience based on John's points?'—or something to that effect."

Of course, it's necessary to manage the question-and-answer part of the presentation so you don't get too far off topic. "If we get off topic, or someone in the audience takes the conversation in a different direction, I might state something like, 'John, we are limited on time, but I would love to address that further. Let's discuss after the presentation,'" says Tom.

Keep in mind that any questions, even if they seem provocative and pessimistic, are signs that your audience is listening. It's better to have an active and engaged audience than an audience that's bored—or worse, sleeping. (It's embarrassing when you hear snoring from the audience!)

No matter how challenging an audience member may be, keep your composure and remain professional.

TIPS FOR ADDRESSING AUDIENCE QUESTIONS

By following some general guidelines, you can successfully manage a question-and-answer session during your presentation. Follow these tips:

Restate the question

If you don't know the answer right away, ask the person to restate the question. This ensures that you correctly understood it, and it buys you additional time to think of a response. It also helps the audience to hear the question, as some might not have heard it initially.

Give your full attention to the person

This shows respect and that you're serious about addressing their question.

Don't assume the audience has heard and understands the question

Not everyone may understand the background information that led to the question. Also, in a large group, often someone may ask a question that the majority of the audience can't hear. If applicable, restate the question in a way so everyone can not only hear it, but also understand it.

Manage the questions

Keep the questions on topic. Don't let those asking questions go too far astray from the central theme. If this happens, you could say something like, "That's a great question, but a little off topic. I'm pleased to discuss that with you further after the presentation," or "That's a question I can't answer quickly. Can we discuss this after the presentation?"

Manage the question session

There may be someone in the audience who dominates the question-and-answer session and feels that all their questions should be given priority. You may need to interrupt that person to give others a chance to ask their questions. You could say, "You have great questions, but let's let others ask questions as well."

Be truthful

Don't lie and pretend to know an answer when you don't; this can negatively affect your credibility. If you don't know the answer, then say so. You might ask if anyone in the audience knows the answer, or you can ask the person if you can get back to them after you've had an opportunity to investigate it. (You may need to ask to get their contact information so you can follow up with them.) You could also refer that person to a source with further information about the topic.

Compliment the questioner

There's always going to be that person whose questions are long, self-important statements. A quick recovery before moving on from the show-off is, "Thank you. Excellent point!"

Be patient

Patience is everything. Don't be so quick to end your time on stage if questions don't come right away. People may be fearful of speaking up or not prepared with questions. Consider telling the audience during or before your summary that you'll be allowing time for questions, and then say, "Now I'm opening it up to questions. Who has the first question?" If no one asks any questions, you might say, "One commonly asked question is, 'How much does all of this cost?'" (Ask whatever common question applies to your topic.) If you voice the first question, then the audience has a model. Hopefully an audience member will pipe up with the next question, but if not, at least one question was asked and answered—even if both the question and answer were from you.

Involve your audience

Depending on the circumstance, if it's a well-informed audience of professionals, consider asking the room if anyone would like to respond to the question. You might also elicit an answer from a specific person (if you know them well enough to comfortably and appropriately do so). For example, "Dr. Smith is our resident advisor on this subject. Dr. Smith, do you mind sharing a few words that address this question?"

PLAN FOR QUESTIONS

Plan and prepare for questions. Consider when and how they'll be addressed. Here are some things to keep in mind when you are planning for audience questions.

Before the presentation

There are a couple of things you can do to prepare for audience questions before your presentation. You can anticipate what your audience's questions will be and lay the ground rules.

Anticipate audience questions

Profile your audience before your presentation to assess and predict their questions. Consider preparing "extra" related slides to show when appropriate that could assist in addressing questions.

Lay the ground rules

Let your audience know at the beginning of your presentation when and how questions will be addressed. State this positively to show that you encourage questions. At certain points during your speech, you might also want to ask the audience if they have any questions regarding what has been addressed so far.

During the Presentation

Consider allowing spontaneous questions during your presentation. Allowing your audience to interact with you throughout your presentation could make a big difference in their interest and retention of your speech. A presentation can be more interesting when the audience participates.

End of the Presentation

If you prefer to allocate questions at the end of your presentation, make sure you set aside sufficient time (typically ten to fifteen minutes should suffice) for questions and limit them as appropriate. Here are some other end-of-presentation question considerations.

Invite follow-up questions

If you have the time after your presentation is over and you're off the stage, offer to address any further questions during that time. Let your audience know where you'll be available.

End with style and dignity

Thank the audience for their time.

CHAPTER 31

The Power of Inspiration and Meditation

Apply techniques to calm yourself
and help you focus.

Before you roll your eyes, consider how a holistic approach to public speaking might work. Meditative or holistic methods can reduce anxiety and improve your focus. The process can consist of a short meditation session prior to your speech, or it may involve other, more strategic methods.

TO START, CONSIDER SOME PREPARATION

Ask these questions when planning your speech:

- What inspires you about your topic?
- What excites you about your topic?

- What's the best part of your message? Why?
- Why do you want to share your message?
- What do you want your audience to know and do with your message?

Understanding the spirit and inspiration of your message will help you better convey that energy in your words and therefore your presentation. Your audience will absorb the energy reflected from you.

DURING THE SPEECH

If you get sidetracked and become anxious, pause and remember why you're inspired by the topic. Then smile. When you smile, your body releases endorphins—brain chemicals known as neurotransmitters—that make you feel happy. They are also natural pain and stress relievers.

Allow yourself to relax and tap into the depths of your inspiration for presenting your message to your audience. Your audience will pick up on your positive energy, receiving your speech with gusto.

If you're unsure how to do this, consider some introspection and self-awareness to get there.

Introspection and self-awareness

Strong speakers present their best self. This requires understanding yourself, knowing what you're skilled at and what you enjoy doing. Start by making a list of all your strong skills and desires. Next consider how you can incorporate these qualities into your presentation. For example, perhaps you're good at getting people to laugh. You could then translate that into injecting humor into a speech.

Perhaps you excel at and enjoy storytelling. This is another method you could apply to a speech.

Going through this process helps you identify traits and talents you can (and should) apply to your speech as well as areas you can improve on. Effective speakers constantly work to capitalize on their strengths and improve their weaknesses.

MEDITATION

If you regularly practice meditation, you probably understand the benefits it reaps. From your experience, you know that meditation can calm nerves and sharpen the mind, and numerous studies back this up. If you're experienced at meditation, I recommend putting it into practice just before you step on the stage to set yourself up to present your most engaging and authentic self. However, if you're new to the practice, test it out prior to your speech. Sit quietly, and for a few minutes, don't do anything but focus on your breath. Do your best to keep your brain from wandering in a million directions. Meditation takes practice, and while this book isn't a guide on how to meditate (there's a plethora of information readily available), even just closing your eyes for a few seconds while breathing in and out deeply and slowly can calm your nerves and center your thoughts.

CHAPTER 32

Strategies for Managing Troublemakers

Don't let any troublemakers ruin your
presentation. Apply simple techniques to keep in
control of your speech.

Even if you're nervous, anxious, excited, or a combination of any of these emotions, you have prepared your speech well and you're ready to go. You take a deep breath, walk up on stage anticipating your speech, and address the audience. And then it happens—you're faced by a skeptical, resistant, or even worse, a hostile audience. The same could happen online; during a live video presentation someone might interrupt your speech with challenging remarks.

Most people are unsure how to effectively handle these situations. They feel accosted, threatened, and embarrassed. It can be easy to take these situations personally.

HOW TO KEEP CALM WHEN FACED WITH A DIFFICULT AUDIENCE

The worst thing you can do is become visibly upset or irritated. Losing your temper will negatively affect your credibility and your power to persuade. Instead, use one of these tactics to manage the situation and take control, turning it to your advantage.

Don't take it personally

Keep in mind that a whole host of factors affect people's feelings and reactions, most of which have nothing to do with you and your speech. Audience members may leave during a presentation because they don't feel well, have to go to the bathroom, have another meeting to attend, or must pick up their child from school. Someone might just be having a bad day, which has nothing to do with you, and feel empowered to react negatively.

Don't get into an argument

Avoid getting defensive when you feel threatened. Some people like to appear as if they're smarter than you. Some also like to actively voice opinions that may not match up with yours. Often these kinds of people are merely looking for attention. However, they may genuinely want to better understand your presentation without ill will. Don't allow either situation to get the best of you by not controlling your emotions. Going head-to-head with someone could turn into a competition that no one will win.

Deflect any negative energy

Don't allow yourself to get upset. When you become aware of your anger, focus on the positive. Tell a joke, smile (not sarcastically, though), and perhaps take a deep breath to help yourself calm down. Maintaining a positive approach will help you redirect your energy to your speech, instead of on the troll.

Address the situation

Acknowledge the individual and address their concerns. Ask questions to gain a further understanding of their situation. If the person has valid points, let them know and even thank them for the information. Your audience will appreciate your willingness to listen and consider new information fairly and reasonably, which can boost your credibility.

Prevent resistance

To prevent and stop resistance, identify the issue and respond with a solution. If you can recognize this early on, you'll have a better chance of avoiding potentially worse issues. Some signs of resistance are obvious, such as when attendees have their heads down looking at cell phones, are sleeping or side-talking, or are staring at you with a glazed, expressionless look on their face. Other signs include folded arms, scowls, ignoring audience-directed questions, and making shocking statements.

Below are some ways you can prevent this kind of resistance.

Keep your audience productive

People can quickly lose interest and become agitated if they have to sit and listen for any period of time, especially if they're minimally interested in the topic. To spark and engage an audience, give them something to do, such as partnering up or working together in small groups to discuss an issue or topic, or responding to a poll during an interactive online presentation.

Avoid confusion

Make sure all instructions are clear, including everything in your speech.

Make it about them

Be clear how your speech benefits the audience. If they don't see the value, then they can easily lose interest and get bored.

Be adaptable

Well-rehearsed speeches may not go as planned due to unforeseen circumstances, such as equipment issues or low audience participation. For example, people may feel more alert and receptive during a morning session and participate enthusiastically yet feel tired and lethargic during a later afternoon session. The same speech given to both sessions may not work as well without some adaptation.

TROUBLESHOOTING TROLLS

Anticipating or faced with trolls in the audience? Here's your guide to managing disruptive attendees during your speech.

Hecklers

Hecklers will interrupt you with inappropriate or aggressive comments that have no obvious point. Hopefully you won't ever have to address this type of person. They can be annoying—not only to you but to the rest of your audience as well. Those focused on what you have to say will appreciate your ability to manage a heckler. They're easy to spot and nearly impossible to avoid.

Don't engage the person; this just gives them fuel to keep going. If possible, ignore them instead. The heckler may give up without being able to elicit any kind of response from you. You could also politely and calmly ask the audience to hold off comments and questions until the end of the speech (which almost always works in this case). One strategy that has worked for me is to walk over to the heckler and stand behind him as I continue speaking to the audience. Breaking eye contact with that person can automatically get them to stop speaking. If the audience is large, you might ask the heckler to identify her or himself. Hecklers may prefer to keep anonymous, so this discourages them from speaking up.

If the situation gets out of hand, you can also politely ask the heckler to leave the room.

Eager Beaver

Some people may simply be very excited about the presentation and can't hold back. This person is often the first to speak up, raise their hand, or offer to help. Embrace this person, as their positive energy can reflect well on the group. Acknowledge their contribution and perhaps ask if anyone else has questions or comments.

Expert

This person challenges your authority in a manner that comes across as if they're the know-it-all and you're a "not know-it-at-all." However, their motives may vary. They may genuinely want to share information and clarify your points, or they may just want some recognition publicly for their expertise in a particular area. Your best offense is a strategic defense in this case. You could ask other members of the audience their opinion to help clarify and validate, resulting in an engaging interaction and discussion among the group. However you handle the situation, make sure you acknowledge the person's comments without getting defensive.

Rambler

We've all experienced this person—the one who goes on and on, telling a story that doesn't really relate to the topic at hand and is not all that interesting. To manage the rambler, cut in, thank them for their comments, and then move on. You could ask for other opinions to deflect the rambling. You could also politely stop them and be honest about having to stick to a strict time schedule. For example, "Very interesting points. I can see how rewarding that must have felt. In the interest of time, though, we're going to need to move on . . ." and then continue with your speech right away before allowing that person a chance to respond.

Dominator

This person likes control and can monopolize any activity. Don't let a dominator take over—it's disrespectful and a waste of everyone's time. Don't react negatively, as the person may have no ill-mannered intentions and may have no idea of their impact. You might encourage them to move the ball back into your court by stating, "Thanks, Robert, now let's hear from . . ." You could also call for a break and speak to that person privately if needed.

Side conversations

In a small venue, people conversing with each other during a presentation is disruptive. At a large venue, it may not be as noticeable, and you could just ignore it. If the side conversation is disruptive, though, treat the situation lightheartedly and sensitively. The people talking may not even be aware that they're being disruptive, and you wouldn't want them to feel bad because that might negatively affect the mood of the room. If necessary, you could ask them to hold their conversation until later. You might even walk up to the chatterers and stand in front of them, not making eye contact, as you continue speaking. They'll instantly get the message.

The Downer

For whatever reason, this person is negative—possibly toward you, the topic, the room, the event, or someone else in the room. They may express their resentment through body language, voice, or by the way they participate (or don't participate). If appropriate, acknowledge the person's concerns either privately or openly. If they're too disruptive, you could ask them to leave or offer to address their concerns at another time.

Complainer

This person likes to complain but has no solutions. If you encourage them, they may keep going with lots of "but . . ." responses. Don't allow yourself to get caught up in this and get off track. Instead briefly acknowledge their issue and then move on.

Negative remarks during live broadcasts

Any live (and recorded) broadcasts open to the public are subject to all kinds of comments. Keep in mind that negative comments with no constructive criticism or good intentions behind them are just empty words.

CHAPTER 33

Using Humor in Your Speech

Anyone can use humor unique to themselves;
you don't have to be a comedian. Appropriate
humor relaxes an audience and makes them feel
comfortable with you as the speaker.

omedian Ellen DeGeneres connects with her audience
through engaging stories and her personable, lighthearted
attitude. She's well known for putting anyone at ease by
building rapport with them, as demonstrated at the commencement speech she gave to Tulane University's graduating class of 2009
where she stated, "Oh boy, thank you, thank you so much. Thank you,
President Cowin. Ah, Mrs. President Cowin. Distinguished guests.
Undistinguished guests. Ah . . . you know who you are. Honored faculty and creepy Spanish teacher. And thank you to all the graduating
class of 2009. I realize most of you are hung over and have splitting

headaches and haven't slept since Fat Tuesday, but you can't graduate until I finish, so listen up."[17]

Ellen captivated the audience effectively with her engaging speech. She could have started in typical fashion, using a more formal, serious tone. However, she used humor to build rapport before addressing the main points of her speech (follow your passion, stay true to yourself, and so on).

You don't have to be a trained comedian to successfully add humor to your speech, but many avoid using humor, fearful of failure and embarrassment. No one wants to tell a joke that flops. If that's you, don't feel pressured (or stressed or worried) that your speech will be a flop without funny puns and witty jokes. You may be more successful delivering a speech in a manner with which you're comfortable—such as one without humor—which will then more likely come across as genuine (another great way to connect with the audience.).

However, some humor, appropriately presented and sprinkled throughout a speech, can be a powerful, valuable, and indispensable tool for getting your message across. Humor can quickly engage an audience and boost your credibility as a speaker. Many corporate leaders, presidents—including former presidents Barack Obama and Abraham Lincoln—and other notables used humor, often making fun of themselves to humanize and connect with the audience.

Consider these benefits of adding humor to your speech:

- Humor relaxes you and the audience.
- Humor helps your audience get a sense of your personality.
- Humor is engaging.
- People may be more likely to remember a funny speech.
- People will be more likely to tell others about a funny speech.
- Humor makes people feel good and happy.

---

17 "Ellen at Tulane Commencement 2009," YouTube, https://www.youtube.com/watch?v=0e8ToRVOtRo.

SHOULD I USE HUMOR?

Use humor if you're comfortable using it and if you think it will captivate and engage your audience and improve your speech. However, humor may not work well in all circumstances; sometimes it's not appropriate to the subject matter or the audience. Consider the following questions when determining whether to use humor.

- Will humor help relax and engage the audience?
- Will the audience be receptive to humor?
- Will the audience be able to understand the meaning and purpose of the humor?
- Might anyone be offended by the humor?
- Would humor detract from my credibility?
- Am I comfortable using humor?

An unreceptive and resistant audience attending your speech in hopes to be convinced otherwise may not appreciate humor. They instead may prefer to learn about hard, credible facts. In contrast, those who are more open and receptive to your topic may appreciate appropriate humor.

HOW CAN I EFFECTIVELY USE HUMOR IN MY SPEECH?

Here are tips for effectively using humor in your speech.

At the right time

Humor—jokes, puns, and rants—shouldn't come across as random, as if you really wanted to share the funny remark but were unsure when to use it. Humor can be used as a lead-in to a key point. For example, you might share a personal story about an embarrassing experience (something the audience can relate to) and then follow it up with ways to prevent something like that from happening again. Humor can also be used spontaneously, as a response to an unexpected experience (like tripping or spilling something on yourself during your presentation) or in response to an audience comment—again, make sure it's appropriate.

Say something original

Overused and common jokes won't likely get the response you'd like. Knock-knock jokes fall into this category. Instead, consider sharing personal stories or stories of others' personal experiences (names not disclosed unless you have permission).

Assess what makes you laugh

Take notes when you hear, see, or read something funny. It could be about anything: animals, people, the weather, business, politics, and so on. Think about what makes you laugh and why it's funny to you. Notice particulars, such as how the person said it, their facial expressions, and the context in which it was said or written (or shown visually). The more we're aware of funny incidents, the easier it can be to recall and share them at the appropriate time.

Write your joke when you feel humorous

It's easier to write humor when you're in a humorous mood. You may find yourself laughing at what you come up with to possibly use in your speech.

Practice

Test your humor on others prior to your speech to get a sense of their reaction and revise as needed. Ask their feedback on why it is or is not funny. When you're confident of the content, practice it until you have it memorized so you don't accidentally forget the punch line in real time.

Relax

Humor should come across naturally, sometimes spontaneously, instead of forced. Think about sharing something humorous that you truly find funny. You'll come across as more genuine.

Keep humor brief

Humor should be used primarily to get the audience's attention and keep them engaged. However, don't spend too much time on it unless that's the key focus and objective of your speech.

Don't give up

Don't worry if humor doesn't come naturally to you. It can take time to develop. Being humorous is a learning process that sometimes works and sometimes doesn't. With practice, you'll find that over time it will get easier to use humor in your presentations.

WHERE TO USE HUMOR IN YOUR SPEECH?

I recommend writing out your speech first before deciding when and where to weave in humor. It will be easier to know when and if you should use humor after you're confident that you have a solid outline reflecting your purpose and key supporting points. After you've written your speech, go through and add in any humor where it might support your points and strategically keep the audience engaged. Review your draft several more times and remove anything that isn't funny or might not be appropriate.

WHAT IF NO ONE LAUGHS?

Don't let the fear that no one will laugh at your jokes stop you from including humor in your speech. Humor can be a very effective way of communicating and connecting with others (i.e., your audience). There are countless stories of professional comedians who bombed on stage. In fact, all professional comedians have told jokes unsuccessfully. Still, they persevered and developed stronger skills from those experiences. So if your audience doesn't laugh, don't fret. Remain calm and confident and just keep going with the rest of your speech as if it was all planned. Your audience may just think you were telling a story.

CHAPTER 34

Preventing and Managing Presentation Mishaps

Don't be caught off guard by unexpected
glitches. Expect the unexpected
and plan accordingly.

K elly (not her real name), a senior manager at Boeing Corporation, was prepared for her speech to other managers and executives at the company. She dressed professionally in a pressed and fitted crème suit and had prepared a polished presentation that began well. Mid-morning, an hour or so after her speech began, she had arranged to have a cup of coffee brought up to her on the platform where she was speaking. With all audience eyes on her, she went to take her first drink, only to find the cap was not secure on the cup and the entire cup of hot coffee spilled down the front of her nearly white suit. The audience's eyes widened and silence filled the room; it was obvious they weren't sure how to react. However, without hesitation, Kelly glanced up after assessing the damage, looked at the audience, smirked, smiled widely, and said, "Well, I guess this is a good time for a break! Let's meet back here in fifteen after I get myself cleaned up." The audience roared with laughter, Kelly regained her composure, and she continued her presentation after the break with confidence in front of a relaxed audience.

Kelly was able to successfully overcome what could have been a presentation disaster. Instead of getting embarrassed, she took advantage of the situation, using it as an opportunity to laugh at herself and connect with her audience. Accidents happen all the time, and we can control how we react—positively or negatively.

Speakers often worry and stress about what might happen, to the detriment of their preparation and presentation. Common questions that might run through a presenter's head include:

- What if I lose my place?
- What if no one laughs at my jokes?
- What if I forget what to say?
- What if I ask a question and no one responds?
- What if I trip and fall?
- What if I sweat profusely?
- What if I'm asked a question I don't have an answer to?
- What if I end too soon or run over too much?

If you have these thoughts, keep in mind that people are human, and your audience likely will be able to relate and empathize if you do something embarrassing. It's not uncommon for a mishap to occur; sometimes they're unavoidable.

Five-time Grammy winner and *New York Times* bestselling author Wynonna Judd captivated her audience with her mesmerizing July 4th "Celebrate America's Birthday" musical outdoor performance in front of a live audience. However, her first song of the night didn't go as planned. The orchestra apparently had their own version of the song, playing it beautifully but not in sync with her singing. Wynonna got a few notes out and then had to stop and ask the orchestra to restart . . . a few times. After several restarts, Wynonna finally gave in to the orchestra and respectfully and enthusiastically asked them to "take it away!" They did, performing a melodic piece. Wynonna didn't walk offstage or cower. Throughout the song, she belted out a few harmonizing notes, as if she were creating the perfect accompaniment on the spot. It worked.

Did she seem embarrassed? Did the mishaps jeopardize her singing career?

Wynonna could have shown anger or embarrassment, or she could have simply said nothing, leaving the audience confused in what might have been an awkward situation. Instead, she connected with the audience through bold and unflinching honesty, keeping them informed of what was happening in a fun and humorous way. She rolled with the punches and kept going, laughing at herself and the situation. Her message conveyed, "Hey, not all things go as planned, but I'm still going to give you a show—so let's go!" Although the performance for that song was clearly not what was intended, she still was able to entertain her audience with beautiful music.

Actress Jennifer Lawrence fell, tripping on her floor-length dress, as she made her way up the stairs from the main floor to the podium on her way to accept her Oscar for Best Actress. She paused momentarily and then quickly picked herself up and made her way to the stage.

She used the fall to connect with the audience, starting her speech with self-deprecating humor, stating, "You guys are just standing up because you feel bad that I fell, and that's really embarrassing, but thank you." She then quickly moved on with her acceptance speech.

Audiences are forgiving. They want you to do well, and they can also relate. If you mess up, they'll probably be silently thinking how glad they are that it wasn't them up there, and they'll respect how well you address the situation.

If you blunder, quickly move on. The audience will too, and then they'll focus on the rest of your presentation.

PRESENTATION MISHAPS GUIDELINES

You can overcome presentation mishaps with ease by keeping in mind the following guidelines.

Be prepared for mishaps and plan accordingly

Consider what might happen and have a backup plan. For example, have a spare battery ready in case your remote pointer battery dies (it's happened to me multiple times), or consider what you would do if your microphone stops working.

Expect mishaps

Mistakes happen to everyone, even those who are well prepared and confident. It's better to accept—and even expect—that you'll make mistakes so you can be better prepared to address them.

Acknowledge the mishap

If your mishap is obvious (such as tripping and falling on stage), acknowledge it. If you don't, your audience may keep on thinking about the mishap instead of focusing on your speech. However, don't make a big deal out of it. A simple "Oops, that was unplanned," or "I'm OK" followed with a smile will suffice; then continue with your speech.

Be human

Laugh at yourself, catch your breath, pause for a moment, and even take a short break, if needed. Allowing yourself to act naturally will help you stay connected with your audience. People will understand and appreciate your candidness.

Practicing your speech is helpful. But memorizing your entire speech, word for word in a specific order and sequence, might trip you up if you forget a step. Your speech could also come across as too rehearsed and dry. Instead, know your topic thoroughly so you can say what you want in many ways.

Keep the momentum going

Although you may feel like running out of the room (or worse, crying), that is, of course, not the wisest option. Instead, briefly acknowledge the mishap and then continue with your speech, picking up where you left off.

PRESENTATION MISHAPS AND SOLUTIONS

Here's a list of common presentation mishaps and what to do about them.

Running out of time

- **Issue:** Professionals are typically sensitive about their time and may quickly become annoyed, affecting your credibility and the success of your speech if you run beyond your scheduled time.

- **Solution:** Practice and time your speech several times until you're comfortable giving it. Also, consider ending it early (about five to ten minutes for a speech scheduled at least twenty minutes long) so you have time for any questions. This also gives you a cushion if you run a few minutes longer than intended.

If you find yourself running out of time, don't rush through to the end. Speaking too quickly can make it difficult for your audience to understand you. Instead, determine the most important key points you want to address and focus on them. Your audience likely won't even know what they're missing, so don't highlight that you're running out of time by explaining what you don't have enough time to tell them. Make sure you leave enough time for the closing portion of your speech; this part shouldn't be left out. The closing portion summarizes your speech and can be your call to action, helping your audience understand why they benefited from your speech and what they need to do with the information going forward.

Forgetting what to say

- **Issue:** Have you ever lost your train of thought, even forgetting what you can usually recall easily? When put on the spot, it's easy to forget the name of your best friend who is standing next to you or your own telephone number. This happens to most everyone, and it can be unnerving when it happens in front of a captive audience, especially in a professional setting. Your speech may be going along smoothly, when your mind suddenly goes blank and you appear dazed and confused. Losing your train of thought happens to a lot of speakers. To turn it around and be successful, you must know how to quickly recover without anyone noticing you got lost.

- **Solution:** To prevent possible slips in thought, know your topic well and practice your speech multiple times. The more comfortable you feel and the more knowledgeable you are about your topic, the more likely you'll be able to recall information without hesitation.

If you still forget what to say next, consider any of these options as appropriate:

- **Make it look planned.** Use the memory lapse as an opportunity to call for a quick break. Your audience won't know any different.

- **Make fun of yourself.** Ask your audience where you left off. Usually, someone in the audience will tell what you were last talking about, which helps you remember your train of thought.

- **Review your notes.** Consider having an outline of your key topics placed somewhere near where you're presenting so you can quickly glance at it if necessary to keep you on track.

Equipment failures

- **Issue:** Despite careful planning, equipment failures are inevitable when it comes to presenting. A battery for your remote may suddenly stop working, you or someone else may forget to bring the correct power cord, or your software isn't compatible with the equipment you're using on-site. Hopefully, any of these situations won't happen to you, but if they do, don't let them ruin your speech.

- **Solution:** Plan and get help. Before you begin your speech, arrange for technical assistance to check your equipment. Also, if possible, arrange for someone to be immediately available to assist with technical issues if they arise during your presentation.

Another solution is to practice and have a backup plan. Avoid being completely reliant on your slides and other visual aids. You should be able to talk about your topic as if you were sharing information directly with a friend in a one-on-one conversation, without using any visual aids.

> ## ⚠ TIP
>
> Know the main points of your presentation. If you run low on time, quickly skim your main points to identify those that are need to know versus nice to know. That way, you can quickly revise and wrap up your speech without sacrificing important content.

If you don't have sufficient time to prepare and rehearse for a speech, then consider printing out your slides or have an outline of your speech prepared before you arrive so you can refer to it if necessary.

Avoid spending too much time during your presentation trying to fix and resolve equipment issues. You'll quickly lose the attention of your audience, and they will become frustrated.

Plenty of things can and will go wrong when speaking in public, but if you expect the unexpected and plan accordingly, you'll be less likely to make mistakes, and you'll be in a better position for reacting well when something does go wrong.

How Well Did You Do? Measuring What Matters

Smiles and head nods are usually telling of an
engaged audience. But is it enough? Did it result
in post presentation sales, action, or change?

ow can you tell if your presentation was successful? Obvious signs are applause, smiles, laughter (at your jokes), questions, accolades, and eye contact. However, to more concretely understand the success of your presentation, you need to consider how you define success relative to the purpose of the speech. Consider these three important questions to measure the success of your speech:

- Did I achieve my objective?
- Did I impact my audience emotionally or intellectually?
- Did the audience remember my message a few days after I spoke?

SUCCESS MEASURE #1: WAS YOUR OBJECTIVE ACHIEVED?

You'll need to review your objective to understand whether you achieved it. Your objective may be easy to measure, such as quantity of books sold, number of enrollments achieved, or amount of surveys completed during the event. Other objectives may be less easily measured, such as tracking whether your message changed people's beliefs and attitudes, although there are ways to understand this as well (read on).

SUCCESS MEASURE #2: DID YOU IMPACT THE AUDIENCE EMOTIONALLY OR INTELLECTUALLY?

Your goal may be to change the way an audience believes, thinks, or feels about a topic. In this case, you might trigger their emotions through inspiration or give them more information, increasing their knowledge about a topic they find useful. How is this measured? Audience feedback.

Audience questions show interest. Their questions mean that they're thinking about your presentation and want to know more. You may also find that people seek you out during or after your talk with comments such as "Great speech" or they share stories related to your speech. These types of comments also indicate their interest in your topic.

SUCCESS MEASURE #3: WHAT DID THE AUDIENCE REMEMBER ABOUT YOUR PRESENTATION?

A speech is a success if the audience positively remembers it after the presentation. However, many, if not most presentations are forgotten within just a few hours. It's important for a speaker to leave a positive, lasting impression that attendees remember.

For example, suppose you gave a presentation about an expensive product or service you sell. Most people probably won't hand over their credit card immediately. They'll need time to think about it. What you want is for them to remember your product or service when it's time for them to decide, thinking, *Yes, let's buy [or act on] this!*

This objective also applies to job interviews. You want the recruiter to positively remember you after the interview (and you may have been one of many other candidates interviewed for the same position), so when it comes time to hire, your name pops up as a strong, viable candidate for further consideration (or even better, the top choice).

METHODS TO MEASURE THE SUCCESS OF A PRESENTATION

There are a variety of methods to measure the success of a presentation. Here are some suggestions.

- **Surveys:** Get feedback from the audience. You could have them complete an end-of-presentation survey (or evaluation) that includes a request for a written description of exactly what they took away from your talk.

- **Bookings:** You know you're outstanding when after your presentation, you're invited to speak at another event.

- **Shared stories:** Audience members approach you during a break or after your presentation and passionately tell you about a related experience they had. This means your message engaged and targeted the audience, who may have been moved by your speech.

- **Sales:** You could track related sales and leads, such as book or product orders, newsletter signups, and business cards handed to you following your presentation. When people want more of what you offer, you know your speech resonated with them and that it was a success.

- **Observations:** Watch how your audience responds to your presentation. Do they appear engaged and interested? Do they ask related questions? Do they actively participate in your presentation activities?

- **Immediate results:** Document any immediate results such as social and news media coverage, follow-up calls, audience questions and comments, and so on.

Presentation Tools

"If you can't explain it simply, you don't
understand it well enough."
—Albert Einstein

Tips for Presenting Well

Here is a quick reference guide to
improve your public speaking.

WHAT NOT TO DO

Avoid these presentation no-nos:

Don't begin with irrelevant banter

Don't start your speech with irrelevant banter and conversational types of questions such as "How's it going today?" or "Hey, how are you all doing?" These kinds of openings add nothing and are awkward for the audience who won't know whether or how to respond.

Don't ramble

Don't ramble, state the obvious, or present a long, drawn-out introduction. You could easily bore and lose your audience if you tell your life story. Instead, keep your introduction concise, engaging, and on point.

Don't ask open-ended questions

Don't ask open-ended questions requiring a verbal response from your audience. Your audience may not know how or whether to respond, and you may end up with no one saying anything or everyone shouting out varying words at the same time. Instead, ask yes or no questions with a show of hands, such as, "Raise your hand if you've ever been to Tanzania."

Don't turn around to read the screen

The audience will be looking at your back, and your voice will project in the wrong direction.

Don't shout over your audience

If the audience gets too loud (i.e., when they're discussing during a group activity in a workshop) and you need to interrupt them, avoid raising your voice. (It's unprofessional to shout at the audience.) Instead, lower your voice. People will begin to go silent so they can hear you.

Don't apologize for anything

Apologizing places emphasis on and directs the audience's attention on whatever you're apologizing for. Your audience may not have even been aware of whatever you felt compelled to address.

WHAT TO DO

Do *all* of the following to ensure your presentations is a success.

Breathe normally

Do a quick breath check. Are you breathing too quickly or not deeply enough? Sometimes pausing to take a deep breath does the trick to calm your nerves.

Welcome everyone

Create an open and welcoming environment. Show your appreciation by genuinely thanking the audience for their time and attention.

Time it

Prepare to end your speech a few minutes before the specified allocated time scheduled. You will have some flexibility and time to address any comments and questions.

Memorize and perfect the first and last thirty seconds of your speech

Your opening and closing are typically the most important parts of your speech. The opening should engage and entice your audience to want to hear and learn more. The last thirty seconds is also important to leave your audience with a final positive impression. The final seconds should be inspiring and memorable.

Make eye contact with the audience

Avoid staring at one or two people. You could make them feel uncomfortable and lose connection with those you don't look at. You don't necessarily have to make eye contact with every person, especially if there are many people in the audience. However, you can scan your eyes back and forth, covering all areas of the room.

Keep pockets empty

Putting your hands in your pockets and fidgeting with your spare change and keys can take the audience's focus off your message.

Talk to your audience, not at them

Tailor your presentation to your audience's interests, and then share the information authentically with them. Don't read your presentation word for word.

Project enthusiasm

Most of communication is nonverbal. How you look and sound are vital, and they communicate your mood. Smile and speak with confidence and enthusiasm. Use natural gestures and voice inflection to add interest to your speech.

Videotape yourself

You may feel somewhat uncomfortable watching yourself, but keep in mind that you're often your worst critic, so you're more likely to notice anything you want to change.

Be prepared to share your contact information

Have available business cards, flyers, and handouts that showcase your work, topic, and you or the business you represent.

Tell a story

Stories can be an effective way of captivating and engaging an audience, especially if the stories are told in a way that's compelling, inspiring, and applicable. Stories can draw the audience in, helping them visualize and understand the point you're making. Stories can also be an effective method of opening a speech; they get your audience interested and set a desired tone.

Be passionate

If you're passionate about something, you'll more likely convey that enthusiasm in your speech and nonverbal movements. Passion drives energy, which is exhilarating not only for you but also for your audience. According to Chris Anderson, curator of the TED conference, who has listened to hundreds of TED presenters, the most successful TED Talks are delivered by speakers who have a passion for their idea and consequently deliver their talks with emotion and imagination. He says, "Your number one task as a speaker is to transfer in your listener's mind an extraordinary gift; a strange and beautiful object that we call an idea."[18]

Be generous

An audience will appreciate and feel positive about a speech that clearly benefits them. Good speakers connect with their audience by genuinely offering something, such as information or services. Motivational speaker Tony Robbins practices this by offering free help and compassion, sharing the spotlight with the audience, and giving credit to others.

Be confident

Even if your knees knock in fright when addressing a live audience, avoid openly telling your audience that you're nervous. They likely won't notice. Instead, show that you're confident. Confidence helps you command the stage and appear credible. Smile, stand up straight, puff out your chest, and look boldly at your audience.

Learn from others

Learn from other speakers, noting what you liked and possibly didn't like about their speech. Notice how and what is said, their nonverbal movements, use of visuals, where they stand, and how well they take command of the stage. Public speaking mentors can be a great resource for learning.

Practice several times

Mark Twain once stated, "It usually takes me more than three weeks to prepare a good impromptu speech." Practice can make the difference between a polished, well-done speech and one that's awkward and painful (for you and your audience). Most of the well-known great

---

18 Chris Anderson, "TED's Secret to Great Public Speaking," TED, April 19, 2016, https://www.youtube.com/watch?v=-FOCpMAww28.

speeches weren't impromptu—they were rehearsed repeatedly until the presenter felt ready.

Slow down

Avoid speaking quickly. You may get through your speech faster, but it will be at the expense of losing your audience who may get bored, annoyed, and give up trying to receive it all. Going fast makes it difficult for your audience to follow and understand what you are saying. Instead, use a steady, deliberate pace—although not too slow. Slowing down also helps you to speak each word clearly and succinctly.

Use silence strategically

Silence can be a powerful tool in public speaking. It signals a pause or moment of transition to the next thought, point, and topic and gives the audience time to digest information. It also can be effectively used to help you regain your train of thought if you get stuck. Instead of using filler words like um and uh to fill gaps in speaking or buy you time as you try to think what to say next, be silent. Your audience won't know that you're stuck, and you'll likely come across as collected and confident.

Promote the Q&A

Many people fear the question-and-answer period at the end of a speech. They worry they won't know the answers, causing them to be embarrassed and appear as a fraud. A student once asked me, "I can practice my speech, but how do I practice unknown answers to unexpected questions?" If you don't know the answer, then admit it (as opposed to pretending you know the answer). Either offer a solution—such as telling them you'll look into it and get back to them—or elicit audience participation, asking if anyone knows the answer.

Revise and rewrite

Avoid crafting a speech that's full of ideas but unclear and unorganized. When you take the time to organize and rewrite, you can produce speeches that flow well, support your purpose, are easy to follow, and are free from errors.

Target and build rapport

The best speakers build rapport with and tailor their messages to their audience. The audience wants to know why they should care and how they'll benefit from the information. Building rapport is about creating trust by identifying similarities, showing the audience that we're like them and share a mutual understanding and interest in the topic. To do this effectively requires knowing as much as you can about your audience before the presentation, including their concerns and motivation triggers. After you know this, you can tailor your speech to them. You can make it about them by using words such as "I understand" and "I emphasize with you."

Use body language strategically

Body language is important for speakers. It's the "tell-tell" of communication and can be used effectively to enhance, reinforce, and clarify a message. Your audience also uses your body language to gauge your credibility. Merely saying, "I'm passionate about this topic" without any inflection and enthusiasm in your voice and no supporting body movements that demonstrate this passion most likely won't be convincing.

Speak from the heart

Just before you begin your speech, take a deep breath and remind yourself that you're presenting what you already know and feel passionate about. Allow that feeling to settle in and forget about all the formalities. You'll be able to speak more freely and fluidly without fear. You'll find that the words easily flow out of your mouth.

Be authentic; be yourself

Avoid trying to be someone you're not. Unless you're a skilled imper-sonator, people may pick up on the fact that you're pretending to be someone else and question your credibility, focusing less on what you say and more on how you say it. You'll be more accepted, respected, and connected with your audience by being authentic and allowing yourself to be vulnerable.

Have fun

Relax and enjoy the process. You've been given a glorious opportu-nity to showcase your great communication skills and help inspire and inform your audience.

Preparation and Evaluation Checklist

Use this checklist as a guide
for preparing and evaluating
your presentation.

Content and Organization

CRITERIA	YES/ NO	COMMENTS/TASKS
Clear and correct		
Appropriate, well targeted to the audience		
Easy to follow		
Key points supported with credible facts		
Smooth transitions between topics		
Logical flow of sections and ideas		

Introduction

CRITERIA	YES/ NO	NOTES/TASKS
Audience greeting		
Attention-getting opening		
Gives a summative overview (pre-view of what you'll talk about)		
Objective/purpose is clear		
Emphasizes audience benefits		
Establishes credibility (of self and organization as applicable)		
Defines key terms necessary for the audience to understand		
States length and acknowledgments		
Provides an overview of any rules (i.e., handling questions, breaks, etc.)		

Body

CRITERIA	YES/NO	COMMENTS/TASKS
Clear		
Includes two to five main points		
Each main point is backed with strong, credible information		
Uses transitional wording to clearly move from one main point to another		

Closing

CRITERIA	YES/NO	COMMENTS/TASKS
Clear takeaway message		
Reinforces the central idea/key message		
Includes a clear call to action		
Summarizes the key points of the speech		

Voice

CRITERIA	YES/ NO	COMMENTS/TASKS
Enunciates clearly with proper pronunciation		
Avoids filler words like *um*, *uh*, and *like*		
Voice is clear and at a good pace		
Avoids jargon		
Varies tone and volume to enhance		

Body Language

CRITERIA	YES/ NO	COMMENTS/TASKS
Maintains eye contact with the audience		
Shows enthusiasm, smiles		
Uses appropriate gestures, no dis-tracting movements		
Stands up straight, facing audience		

Visual Aids

CRITERIA	YES/ NO	COMMENTS/TASKS
Clear, not overcrowded		
Visual aids are easy for the audience to understand		
Is appropriately used with media		
No spelling and grammar errors		
Managed seamlessly with oral speech		
Enhances and helps clarify oral speech		
Easy to see by entire audience or from any point in the room where the audience is located		

General

CRITERIA	YES/ NO	COMMENTS/TASKS
Adheres to time limit		
Manages questions well		
Appears comfortable with the audience (use of visual aids, gestures, stance, and eye contact are natural and fluid)		
Has a strong command and knowledge of the information		
Uses effective methods to engage the audience throughout the speech		

Venue/Location

CRITERIA	YES/ NO	COMMENTS/TASKS
Event is large enough to accommodate audience (room capacity)		
Provides access to equipment needed, including microphone, overhead projector, computer equipment, and extension cords		
Can control the ambiance (curtains, blinds, lighting)		
Noise distractions are managed or removed		
Presentation accommodates seating arrangement		
Refreshments provided if applicable		
Availability and location of lectern or table known, if applicable		
Venue is handicap accessible (as applicable)		

Live Video Streaming/Webcasts

CRITERIA	YES/NO	COMMENTS/TASKS
Knows how to use the software		
Has a backup plan in case the software doesn't work		
Background supports and enhances, not distracts from speaker (no clutter, messes, and inappropriate visuals such as signs, pictures, etc.)		
Room well set up for optimal audio (sounds aren't muffled and distorted)		
Background noise limited or removed		
Appearance appropriate (well-groomed and dressed for the occasion)		
Uses good lighting (speaker well illuminated and not shadowed)		
Well positioned in front of the camera (easily seen by the audience)		
Eye contact is at the same level of the camera		
Clear instructions for participants (includes use of the software)		
Uses a quality microphone		
Smiles throughout		
Speaks clearly		

Author's Note

Effective public speaking is both an art and a skill, requiring mindfulness and creativity, that can be learned and developed. The process can be a fun and stimulating experience that will empower you in any boardroom or public presentation. It can give you the confidence you need to achieve the higher success that you want.

Simply by learning and applying some simple tools for delivering a compelling and dynamic speech, you can effect great change in both your professional and personal life.

I wish you the best on your path of success!

—Lisa Kleiman

Resources

1994 Inaugural Address, Cape Town. (n.d.). Retrieved from Genius: https://genius
.com/Nelson-mandela-1994-inaugural-address-cape-town-annotated

5 secrets of a successful TED Talk. (Science of People). Retrieved from Science of
People: http://www.scienceofpeople.com/2015/03/secrets-of-a-successful-ted-talk/

5 things that make the Gettysburg address so powerful. (n.d.). Retrieved from Speak
Like a Pro: http://www.speaklikeapro.co.uk/Gettysburg.htm

5 tips on how to present like Steve Jobs. (2012, May). Retrieved from Entrepreneur:
https://www.entrepreneur.com/article/223513

Abigail Tenembaum, M. W. (2018, Jan. 10). *Why Oprah's talk works: Insight from a
TED speaker coach*. Retrieved from Ted Blog: https://blog.ted.com/why-oprahs-talk
-works-insight-from-a-ted-speaker-coach/

About Dr. King. (n.d.). Retrieved from The King Center: http://www.thekingcenter
.org/about-dr-king

Abraham Lincoln as a Speaker. (n.d.). Retrieved from Abraham Lincoln Online:
http://www.abrahamlincolnonline.org/lincoln/speeches/speaker.htm

Agrawal, A. (2016, March 11). *5 Tips to Give a Top Online Sales Presentation*.
Retrieved from Salesforce.com: https://www.salesforce.com/blog/2016/03/5-tips-to
-give-a-top-online-sales-presentation.html

Alton, L. (2018, June 7). *How to Flatter Your Target Audience (and Why You Should)*.
Retrieved from Inc.com: https://www.inc.com/larry-alton/how-to-flatter-your
-target-audience-and-why-you-should.html

Analysis of a speech by Oprah Winfrey. (2018). Retrieved from Manner of Speaking:
https://mannerofspeaking.org/2018/01/08/analysis-of-a-speech-by-oprah-winfrey/

Analysis of Nelson Mandel's Inauguration Speech. (n.d.). Retrieved from Marked by Teachers: http://www.markedbyteachers.com/university-degree/media-studies /analysis-of-nelson-mandela-s-inauguration-speech.html

Anderson, C. (2016, April). *TED's secret to great public speaking.* Retrieved from YouTube: https://www.youtube.com/watch?v=-FOCpMAww28

Arnold, K. (2010). *Boring to Bravo: Proven Presentation Techniques to Engage, Involve, and Inspire Your Audience to Action.* Greenleaf Book Group Press, 1 edition.

Aviva Musicus, A. T. (2014). *Eyes in the Aisles, Why Is Cap'n Crunch Looking Down at My Child?, .* Environment and Behavior.

Bedrick, S. (2013, Aug.). *Why has the "I Have a Dream" Speech been so Successful?* Retrieved from blog.toastspot: http://blog.toastspot.com/blog/why-has-the-i-have -a-dream-speech-been-so-successful

Berger, B. (n.d.). *Abraham Lincoln the Man.* Retrieved from National Park Service: https://www.nps.gov/linc/learn/historyculture/abraham-lincoln-the-man.htm

Bilanich, B. (n.d.). *Michelle Obama - Public Speaking 101.* Retrieved from Budbilanich.com: http://www.budbilanich.com/michelle-obama-public -speaking-101

Bill Clinton and the art of speaking in a "human voice." (2006, October). Retrieved from Presentation Zen: http://www.presentationzen.com/presentationzen/2006/10 /bill_clinton_an.html

Bodie, G. D. (2009). *A Racing Heart, Rattling Knees, and Ruminative Thoughts: Defining, Explaining, and Treating Public Speaking Anxiety.* Communication Education.

Caffrey, A. (2018, Jan). *Award Speeches.* Retrieved from Public Speaking Expert: http://www.publicspeakingexpert.co.uk/AwardSpeeches.html

Cameron, D. (n.d.). *Speeches.* Retrieved from Winston Churchill: https://www .winstonchurchill.org/resources/speeches/

Canal, E. (2018). *Oprah Winfrey Nailed Every Public Speaking Lesson You Could Learn in Her Golden Globes Speech.* Retrieved from Inc.com: https://www.inc.com/emily -canal/oprah-winfrey-golden-globes.html

Carr, C. (2015, Jan.). *What Made "I Have a Dream" such a Perfect Speech.* Retrieved from Fast Company: http://www.fastcompany.com/3040976/what-made-i-have-a -dream-such-a-perfect-speech

Closing Quotes. (n.d.). Retrieved from Brainy Quote: http://www.brainyquote.com /quotes/keywords/closing.html

Components of a Speech. (n.d.). Retrieved from Boundless Communications: https: //courses.lumenlearning.com/boundless-communications/chapter/components-of -a-speech/

Conducting a Q&A Session. (2016, August 18). Retrieved from Boundless Communications: https://www.boundless.com/communications/textbooks /boundless-communications-textbook/delivering-the-speech-12/managing-q-a-68 /conducting-a-q-a-session-268-4213/

Croston, G. (2012, Nov. 29). *The Thing We Fear More Than Death.* Retrieved from Psychology Today: https://www.psychologytoday.com/us/blog/the-real-story -risk/201211/the-thing-we-fear-more-death

Croxton, J. (2017, March). *How To Start A Presentation Tips And Tricks – 22 Powerful Strategies.* Retrieved from Custom Show: https://www.customshow.com/start -presentation-tips-tricks/

Cuddy, A. (2012, June). *Your body language shapes who you are.* Retrieved from TED. com: http://www.ted.com/talks/amy_cuddy_your_body_language _shapes_who_you_are?utm_medium=on.ted.com-none&awesm=on.ted.com _d0Ivd&utm_campaign=&utm_source=direct-on.ted .com&share=1c3432f326&utm_content=roadrunner-rrshorturl

Daum, K. (n.d.). *10 tips for giving great online presentations.* Retrieved from Inc.com: https://www.inc.com/kevin-daum/10-tips-for-giving-great-online-presentations .html

Daum, K. (n.d.). *Inc.com.* Retrieved from 10 Tips for giving great online presentations: https://www.inc.com/kevin-daum/10-tips-for-giving-great-online- presentations.html.

Decker, B., & Decker, K. (2012, Dec.). *The Top Ten and Best (and Worst) Communicators of 2012.* Retrieved from Decker Communications: https://decker.com

Degeneres, E. (2012, June). *Living Life with Integrity*. Retrieved from Trend hunter: http://www.trendhunter.com/keynote/motivational-commencement-speech

Detz, J. (2002). *How to Write and Give a Speech*. New York: St. Martin's Press.

Dlugan, A. (2011, Dec.). "How to Stop Saying Um, Uh, and Other Filler Words." http://sixminutes.dlugan.com/stop-um-uh-filler-words/.

Dlugan, A. (2007, Nov.). *Learn the Perfect Q&A*. Retrieved from Sixminutes: http://sixminutes.dlugan.com/leading-the-perfect-qa/

Dockter, W. (2015, Jan). *Winston Churchill's 10 most important speeches*. Retrieved from The Telegraph: http://www.telegraph.co.uk/news/winston-churchill/11366880/Winston-Churchills-10-most-important-speeches.html

Doyle, A. (2017, Dec. 6). *Elevator Pitch Examples and Writing Tips*. Retrieved from Thebalance: https://www.thebalance.com/elevator-speech-examples-and-writing-tips-2061976

Driscoll, D. L. (n.d.). https://owl.english.purdue.edu/owl/owlprint/652/. Retrieved from OWL Purdue: https://owl.english.purdue.edu/owl/owlprint/652/

Effective Vocal Delivery. (2016, May). Retrieved from Boundless Communications: https://www.boundless.com/communications/textbooks/boundless-communications-textbook/delivering-the-speech-12/effective-vocal-delivery-64/pitch-255-4173/

Feloni, R. (2016, March). *Tony Robbins breaks down his top 3 public speaking techniques*. Retrieved from Business Leader: http://www.businessinsider.com/tony-robbins-public-speaking-tips-2016-3

Figure 1. (n.d.). Retrieved from Roylty Free, CC-BY: http://401kcalculator.org

Five tips for organizing your speech. (n.d.). Retrieved from Teacher Joe: http://www.teacherjoe.us/PublicSpeaking04.html

Frum, D. (2000). *How We Got Here: The '70's*. New York: Basic Books.

Gallo, C. (2012, Oct.). *11 Presentation lessons you can stil learn from Steve Jobs*. Retrieved from Forbes: http://www.forbes.com/sites/carminegallo/2012/10/04/11-presentation-lessons-you-can-still-learn-from-steve-jobs/#4818bcd71516

Gallo, C. (2014, Jan. 8). *Keynotes: Public Speaking Lessons From Marissa Mayer and John Chambers.* Retrieved from Forbes: http://www.forbes.com/sites /carminegallo/2014/01/08/ces-keynotes-public-speaking-lessons-from-marissa -mayer-and-john-chambers/#78d7ce6c4905

Gallo, C. (2014, Nov.). *Steve Jobs and Winston Churchill Didn't Start Out as Great Speakers.* Retrieved from Forbes.com: http://www.forbes.com/sites /carminegallo/2014/11/25/steve-jobs-and-winston-churchill-didnt-start-out-as -great-speakers/#1408587b580a

Gallo, C. (2016, April 11). *The simple, 3-step formula that made Steve Job's speeches so compelling.* Retrieved from Business Insider: http://www.businessinsider.com/steve-jobs-followed-a-simple-3-step-formula-for-all-of-his-speeches-2016-4

Genard, G. (2016, Jan.). *Speak for Success!* Retrieved from Genard Method: https:// www.genardmethod.com/blog/bid/142073/grab-your-audience-12-foolproof-ways -to-open-a-speech

Gibbs, N. (2008). *When New President Meets Old, It's Not Always Pretty.* Retrieved from Time: http://content.time.com/time/politics/article/0,8599,1857862,00.html

Gimmicks. (n.d.). Retrieved from Your Dictionary: Your dictionary, ://www .yourdictionary.com/gimmick#BV24ga5kI8Og2x87.99

Greene, R. (2015, Jan.). *The 7 reasons why JFK is one of the world's greatest speakers, and what we can learn from him.* Retrieved from The Huffington Post: http://www .huffingtonpost.com/richard-greene/the-7-reasons-why-jfk-is-_b_6200548.html

Greetham, C. (2017). Director, Boeing.

Griffiths, S. (2014, Nov.). *The sound of STATUS: Powerful people develop loud, high-pitched, monotonous voices, study claims.* Retrieved from Daily Mail: http://www .dailymail.co.uk/sciencetech/article-2847208/The-sound-STATUS-Powerful -people-develop-loud-high-pitched-monotonous-voices-study-claims.html

Harrison, K. (2015, Jan. 20). *A Good Presentation is About Data and Story.* Retrieved from Forbes: Forbes.com

Hart, K. (2016, Feb.). *10 powerful pubic speaking tips.* Retrieved from Speakerhub: https://www.slideshare.net/SpeakerHub/10-powerful-public-speaking-tips-from -some-of-the-best-speakers-in-the-world

Heneghan, C. (2015, Dec.), *'Give them a rich experience': The importance of retaining customer loyalty*. Retrieved from FoodDive: https://www.fooddive.com/news/give-them-a-rich-experience-the-importance-of-retaining-customer-loyalty/410314/

His Speeches: How Churchill Did It. (n.d.). Retrieved from The Churchill Centre: http://www.winstonchurchill.org/resources/speeches/speeches-about-winston-churchill/his-speeches-how-churchill-did-it

How Good Are Your Presentation Skills? (n.d.). Retrieved from Mind Tools: https://www.mindtools.com/pages/article/newCS_96.htm

How to give an unforgettable wedding toast. (2018, Jan.). Retrieved from Shutterfly: https://www.shutterfly.com/ideas/wedding-toasts/

How to nail your bridesmaid or maid of honor speech. (n.d.). Retrieved from The Knot: https://www.theknot.com/content/wedding-toasting-tips-for-the-maid-of-honor

How to write a speech. (n.d.). Retrieved from Write out loud: https://www.write-out-loud.com/howtowritespeech.html

Hsu, J. (2008, August 1). *The Secrets of Storytelling: Why We Love a Good Yarn*. Retrieved from Scientific American: http://www.scientificamerican.com/article/the-secrets-of-storytelling/

Inzunza, V. (2012, Dec. 3). *History's Greatest Speakers and Their Greatest Speeches*. Retrieved from Pencils.com: http://pencils.com/historys-greatest-speeches/

Iselin, T. (2017). *Principal and Founder, First Things First*. (L. Kleiman, Interviewer)

James, G. (n.d.). *9 Rules for Online Sales Presentations*. Retrieved from Inc.com: https://www.inc.com/geoffrey-james/9-rules-for-online-sales-presentations.html

Janssens, C. (n.d.). *How to Give a Great Speech*. Retrieved from Christiaan Janssens: https://christiaan-janssens.blogspot.com/2013/05/how-to-give-great-speech.html

John F. Kennedy. (n.d.). Retrieved from Obama White House: https://obamawhitehouse.archives.gov/1600/presidents/johnfkennedy

John F. Kennedy. (n.d.). Retrieved from The White House: https://www.whitehouse.gov/about-the-white-house/presidents/john-f-kennedy/

Jr., B. M. (2014, Jan. 28). *Things Great Speakers Always Do*. Retrieved from Inc.com: https://www.inc.com/bill-murphy-jr/9-things-great-speakers-always-do.html

Keynote Speakers. (n.d.). Retrieved from Keynotes: http://www.keynotes.org/speaker/

Khoury, P. (n.d.). *4 Things that Can go Wrong with your Presentation and how to Handle Them*. Retrieved from Magnetic Speaking: https://magneticspeaking.com/4-things -that-can-go-wrong-with-your-presentation-and-how-to-handle-them/

Know your audience. (n.d.). Retrieved from Speech Tips: http://www.speechtips.com /audience.html

Kogekar, H. (2012, Feb. 07). *Think Tank: An elevator pitch for your project*. Retrieved from CIO: https://www.cio.com.au/article/414586/think_tank_an_elevator_pitch _your_project/

Kolowich, L. (2014, Feb.). *8 Ways to Make Your Online Sales Presentations More Like Face-to-Face Meetings*. Retrieved from Insight Squared: http://www.insightsquared .com/2014/02/8-ways-to-make-your-online-sales-presentations-more-like-face-to -face-meetings/

Krampe, J. (2013, Nov). *Ryan Seacrest's 4 Secrets for a Great Interview*. Retrieved from success.com: http://www.success.com/article/ryan-seacrests-4-secrets-for-a-great -interview

Kusnet, D. (2012, Sept. 7). *How Bill Clinton Ad-libs his Way to a Winning Speech*. Retrieved from CNN.com: http://www.cnn.com/2012/09/06/opinion/kusnet -clinton-speech-style/index.html

Landrum, M. (n.d.). *Speaking Eye to Eye*. Retrieved from Toastmasters: https://www .toastmasters.org/magazine/articles/speaking-eye-to-eye

Leanne, S. (2008). *Say It Like Obama: The Power of Speaking with Purpose and Vision*. McGraw-Hill.

Lee, M. (2017, Feb. 26). *8 Creative Ways to Use Live-Streaming for B2B Brands*. Retrieved from Social Media Today: https://www.socialmediatoday.com /marketing/8-creative-ways-use-live-streaming-b2b-brands

M., E. (n.d.). *Presenting Facts and Figures Clearly and Effectively*. Retrieved from Modicum: https://modicum.agency/blog/presenting-facts-and-figures-clearly-and -effectively/

Madison, L. (2012, June). *Remembering Reagan's "Tear Down This Wall" speech 25 years later*. Retrieved from CBS News: http://www.cbsnews.com/news/remembering -reagans-tear-down-this-wall-speech-25-years-later

Majumdar, A. (2014, Feb.). *How to create and present a highly effective webinar*. Retrieved from Elearning Industry: https://elearningindustry.com/14-tips-to-create -and-present-a-highly-effective-webinar

Making the "Un-Presentation". (2003). Retrieved from The Total Communicator: http://totalcommunicator.com/chat_article.html

Mazur, M. (2013, Nov.). *4 Essential Ingredients to Creating an Epic Audience Experience*. Retrieved from Communication Rebel: https://drmichellemazur .com/2013/11/4-essential-ingredients-to-creating-an-epic-audience-experience.html

McAdams, J. (2016). *Eisenhower's Farewell Address to the Nation*. The Kennedy Assassination.

McCoy, J. (n.d.). *Impromptu and Extemporaneous Speeches*. Retrieved from Slide Player: http://slideplayer.com/slide/4737514/

McGarrity, M. (2018, Jan. 12). *A Speech Coach Explains Exactly Why Oprah Sounded So Presidential*. Retrieved from QZ.com: https://qz.com/1178889/a-speech -coach-explains-exactly-why-oprah-winfreys-golden-globes-speech-sounded-so -presidential/

McGonigal, J. (2012, June). *TED Global 2012–The game that can give you 10 extra years of life*. Retrieved from TED.com: https://www.ted.com/talks/jane_mcgonigal _the_game_that_can_give_you_10_extra_years_of_life?language=en#t-35229

Meikle, G. (2014, Jan). *Effective Hand Gestures for Better Presentations*. Retrieved from Inter-Activ: https://www.inter-activ.co.uk/presentation-skills/effective-hand -gestures/

Michelle Obama's full DNC speech. (2012, Sept. 5). Retrieved from The Washington Post: https://www.washingtonpost.com/video/politics/first-lady-michelle-obama -addresses-the-democratic-national-convention/2012/09/05/2d9e3de4-f6e7-11e1 -8253-3f495ae70650_video.html?utm_term=.3e5cd1c19d60

Milburn, J. (2010). *Papers Shed Light on Eisenhower's Farewell Address*. The Huffington Post.

Moore, D. (n.d.). *4 Qualities of Amazing Public Speakers*. Retrieved from The Muse: https://www.themuse.com/advice/4-qualities-of-amazing-public-speakers

Moran, G. (2016, Feb.). *7 habits of the best public speakers*. Retrieved from Fast Company: http://www.fastcompany.com/3057007/how-to-be-a-success-at-everything/7-habits-of-the-best-public-speakers

Morgan, N. (2008, April). *Body Language*. Retrieved from Public Words: http://www.publicwords.com/2008/04/18/body-language-5/

Morgan, N. (2012, June). *Body language: how to master non-verbal communication*. Retrieved from Public Words: http://wwwpublicwords.com/2012/06/26/body-language-how-to-master-non-verbal-communication/

Murphy, B. (n.d.). *9 things great speakers always do*. Retrieved from Inc.com: https://www.inc.com/bill-murphy-jr/9-things-great-speakers-always-do.html

NACE. (2016). *Job Outlook 2016*. National Association of College and Employers.

National Churchill Museum. (n.d.). Retrieved from Winston Churchill's Speeches: https://www.nationalchurchillmuseum.org/winston-churchills-speeches.html

Naughton, J. (2011, Oct.). *Steve Jobs: Stanford commencement address*, June 2005. Retrieved from The Guardian: https://www.theguardian.com/technology/2011/oct/09/steve-jobs-stanford-commencement-address

Nelson Mandela quotes: A collection of memorable words from former South African president. (2013, Dec.). Retrieved from CBS News: https://www.cbsnews.com/news/nelson-mandela-quotes-a-collection-of-memorable-words-from-former-south-african-president/

Nelson Mandela: Lesson for Future Orators. (n.d.). Retrieved from Princeton Public Speaking: http://princetonpublicspeaking.com/public-speaking-tips/nelson-mandela-public-speaking/

Nelson Mandel's Inaugural Address as President of South Africa. (1994). Retrieved from Blackpast.org: http://www.blackpast.org/1994-nelson-mandela-s-inaugural-address-president-south-africa-0#sthash.ZLVnenpQ.dpuf

Nonverbal Delivery Tips. (n.d.). Retrieved from Speaking in the Disciplines: http://www.speaking.pitt.edu/student/public-speaking/suggestions-nonverbal.html

Non-Verbal Interviewing Skills. (n.d.). Retrieved from Salisbury: http://www
.salisbury.edu/careerservices/students/Interviews/NonVerbal.html

Oates, D. (2016, Aug.). *Why Michelle Obama is a Great Speaker*. Retrieved from
Stalwartcom.com: http://stalwartcom.com/blog/why-michelle-obama-is-a-great
-speaker/

Ogorodney, I. (2014, Nov 7). *25 Things you Probably Didn't Know About the Berlin
Wall*. Retrieved from rt.com: https://www.rt.com/news/20155-berlin-wall
-anniversary-25/

Opening your presentation. (n.d.). Retrieved from Presentation Skills Success: http://
presentation-skills-success.com/Opening_your_presentation.html

Oprah Winfrey's Speech Analysis. (2018). Retrieved from Success Strategies: https://
www.successstrategies.com/oprah-winfreys-speech-analysis/

Phillips, B. (2014, Jan. 15). *The Television Host I Admire the Most*. Retrieved from Mr.
Media Training: http://www.mrmediatraining.com/2014/01/15/the-television-host
-i-admire-the-most/

Pierce, S. (2007, July). *The Perfect Presentation: Materials*. Retrieved from
Entrepreneur: https://www.entrepreneur.com/article/181172

Pink, D. (2009, Aug.). *The Puzzle of Motivation*. Retrieved from YouTube: https://
www.youtube.com/watch?v=rrkrvAUbU9Y

Pitch. (n.d.). Retrieved from Encyclopedia Britannica: https://www.britannica.com
/topic/pitch-speech

Preparing a Presentation. (n.d.). Retrieved from Skills You Need: https://www
.skillsyouneed.com/present/prepare-presentation.html

Presentations in Interviews. (n.d.). Retrieved from Skills You Need: https://www
.skillsyouneed.com/present/interview-presentations.html

Public Speaking Tools and Props. (n.d.). Retrieved from Speech Tips: http://www
.speechtips.com/public-speaking-tools-speech-props.html

Public Speaking: Practice and Ethics. (n.d.). Retrieved from Lardbucket.org:
https://2012books.lardbucket.org/books/public-speaking-practice-and-ethics/s12
-introductions-matter-how-to-be.html

Rezvani, S. (n.d.). *Four Ways to Stop Saying "Um" and Other Filler Words*. Retrieved from Forbes: http://www.forbes.com/sites/work-in-progress/2014/12/17/four-ways -to-stop-saying-um-and-other-filler-words/#9bc5a7653c59

Ryan Seacrest. (n.d.). Retrieved from People, Time Inc.: 1. http://www.people.com /people/ryan_seacrest/biography/0,,20164719_10,00.html

Sandberg, S. (2013). *Lean In: Women, Work, and the Will to Lead*. New York: Alfred Knopf.

Schramm, J. (August 20, 2014). *How to Present to a Small Audience*. Retrieved from Harvard Business Review: https://hbr.org/2014/08/how-to-present-to-a-small- audience#

Segal, Z. *Getting There: A Book of Mentors*. New York: Abrams Image.

Sevenson, S. (2012, Oct.). *Simplicity and Order for All*. Retrieved from The Wall Street Journal: http://www.wsj.com/articles/SB10001424052970204425904578072 640691246804

Sheelenbarger, S. (April, 2013). *Is This How You Really Talk?* Retrieved from The Wall Street Journal: http://www.wsj.com/articles/SB10001424127887323735604578440 851083674898

Sinek, S. (2009, Sept.). *How Great Leaders Inspire Action*. Retrieved from TED.com: http://www.ted.com/talks/simon_sinek_how_great_leaders_inspire_action

Smith, J. (2015, June 30). *Brilliant Ways to Start a Presentation*. Retrieved from Business Insider: 1. http://www.businessinsider.com/best-ways-to-start-a -presentation-2015-6

Smith, K. (2017, Sept. 28). *Get An Elevator Pitch That Sounds Like You AND Gets You The Job*. Retrieved from Skillcrush: https://skillcrush.com/2015/05/08/elevator -pitch-proud-of/

Snippe, E. (2016, April). *10 Powerful Public Speaking Tips from Some of the Best Speakers in the World: 60-second summary*. Retrieved from Speakerhub: https:// speakerhub.com/blog/10-powerful-public-speaking-tips-some-best-speakers -world-60-second-summary

Sobocan, C. (2013, April). *Public Speaking Tips (from Bill Clinton)*. Retrieved from Raise Your Voice: http://www.raiseyourvoicecoaching.com/public-speaking-tips -from-bill-clinton/

Steve Jobs. (n.d.). Retrieved from Forbes: http://www.forbes.com/profile/steve-jobs/

Strang, T. (2015, Oct.). *Five Guidelines for Effective Online Presentations*. Retrieved from Cengage/Professional Development and Training: https://blog.cengage.com /five-guidelines-for-effective-online-presentations/

Street, E. (2015, Jan. 7). *Overcoming Obstacles: What Oprah Winfrey Learned From Her Childhood of Abuse*. Retrieved from Learning Liftoff: https://www.learningliftoff. com/overcoming-obstacles-what-oprah-winfrey-learned-from-her-abusive -childhood/

Taylor, D. (2016, Sept. 8). *How (and how not) to give great birthday toasts*. Retrieved from Hallmark.com: https://ideas.hallmark.com/articles/birthday-ideas /birthday-toasts/

Taylor, D. (2012, Dec.). *How to Give a Good Presentation Online*. Retrieved from Wordpress: https://donaldhtaylor.wordpress.com/2012/12/06/how-to-give-a-good -presentation-online/

The 30-Second Rule: How to Create Unforgettable Presentations. (n.d.). Retrieved from Peter Economy Inc.: http://www.inc.com/peter-economy/the-30-second-rule-how -to-create-unforgettable-presentations.html

The Advantages and Disadvantages of PowerPoint. (2016, May 26). Retrieved from Boundless: https://www.boundless.com/communications/textbooks/boundless -communications-textbook/preparing-and-using-visual-aids-16/using-powerpoint -and-alternatives-successfully-85/the-advantages-and-disadvantages-of -powerpoint-323-5654/

The World's Most Powerful People, #64 Bill Clinton. (n.d.). Retrieved from Forbes: http://www.forbes.com/profile/bill-clinton/

Top 10 Most Powerful Orators Of The 20th Century. (n.d.). Retrieved from Techno Crazed: http://www.technocrazed.com/top-10-most-influential-and-powerful -orators-of-21st-century-videos

Torok, G. (n.d.). *Top 10 tips on how to open your speech*. Retrieved from Speech Coach for Executives: http://www.speechcoachforexecutives.com/article_21.html

Tsaousides, T. (2017, November 17). *Why Are We Scared of Public Speaking?* Retrieved from Psychology Today: https://www.psychologytoday.com/us/blog/smashing-the-brainblocks/201711/why-are-we-scared-public-speaking

Unknown. (n.d.). *Crafting an Elevator Pitch.* Retrieved from MindTools: https://www.mindtools.com/pages/article/elevator-pitch.htm

Unknown. (n.d.). *Elevator Pitch.* Retrieved from Oxford University Presents: http://www.oxfordpresents.com/ms/jack/elevator/

Unknown. (2017, March 20). *Elevator Pitch Examples from Successful Startups.* Retrieved from Slidebean: https://slidebean.com/blog/startups/elevator-pitch-examples

Up, J. (2011). *50 Years Later, We're Still Ignoring Ike's Warning.* The Washington Post.

Up, J. (2008). *Military-Industrial Complex Speech*, Dwight D. Eisenhower, 1961. Avalon Project.

Verderber, R., Verderber, K., & Sellnow, D. (2016). *COMM 4.* Boston: Cengage Learning.

Wedding Toasts. (n.d.). Retrieved from Wedding paper divas: https://www.weddingpaperdivas.com/wedding-toasts.htm

What made John F. Kennedy a good public speaker? (n.d.). Retrieved from Reference: https://www.reference.com/history/made-john-f-kennedy-good-public-speaker-70f4c8a25c4deeed

Williams, R. (2013, Dec.). *Why Nelson Mandela Was a Great Leader.* Retrieved from Psychology Today: https://www.psychologytoday.com/blog/wired-success/201312/why-nelson-mandela-was-great-leader

withheld, C. (2017). Director, Boeing Company. (L. Kleiman, Interviewer)

withheld, M. (2017). COO (company name witheld). (L. Kleiman, Interviewer)

Wrench, R. (2016). *Energy Consultant, Retired; Aerospace Scientist.* (L. Kleiman, Interviewer)

About the Author

Lisa Kleiman has coached individuals and facilitated hundreds of classes, workshops, and seminars for diverse audiences across the globe on such topics as public speaking, business writing, business and managerial communication, English as a second language, and English composition. She has held management and consulting positions at Fortune 500 companies and has served as a faculty member teaching undergraduate and graduate courses.

Lisa is a self-proclaimed public introvert with a passion for communication and helping others develop their presence and voice with clarity, confidence, and authenticity in both written and oral formats. She is an academic scholar with an education specialist degree in adult and organizational learning and leadership, a master of English concentration in technical and professional communication, and a bachelor of science degree in marketing and management with academic and professional certificates in human resources and records management.

9 781632 992321